HARDPRESS.NET
HOME OF HARD-TO-FIND BOOKS

Lectures and Essays: Ireland and the Irish. the Worth of Liberty. True Manhood. the Pulpit. Patriotism. Economies. Music. the Young Musician. a Day in Springfield. Chatterton. Carlyle. Savage and Dermody
by Henry Giles

Address:
HardPress
8345 NW 66TH ST #2561
MIAMI FL 33166-2626
USA
Email: info@hardpress.net

LECTURES AND ESSAYS.

BY

HENRY GILES.

IN TWO VOLUMES.
VOLUME II.

BOSTON:
TICKNOR, REED, AND FIELDS.
M DCCC L.

Entered according to Act of Congress, in the year 1850, by
TICKNOR, REED, AND FIELDS,
In the Clerk's Office of the District Court of the District of
Massachusetts.

BOSTON:
THURSTON, TORRY, AND COMPANY,
31 Devonshire Street.

CONTENTS.

LECTURES AND ESSAYS.

IRELAND AND THE IRISH,

IN 1848.

THE three journals named below are in opposition to the British government in Ireland, but with different degrees of antagonism. "The Tablet" is a paper in the interest of the Roman Catholic Church, and though English in its spirit and editorship, it sympathizes with the struggles going forward in Ireland. It denounces the Union, it pleads for Repeal; but it does not commit itself to any danger of legal prosecution.

"The Nation" is a journal pledged violently to more than Repeal, — peaceably if possible, forcibly if it must be. It contains much spirited writing, and reports of speeches, that defy the legal authorities, and despise all compromise. This is the organ of " Young Ireland," and of a portion of the physical-force party. Still, though it hints at republicanism, it does not openly avow it. It professes loyalty to the imperial crown, but disowns the right of the imperial legislature to make laws for Ireland. The real purport of its views is, not simply repeal of the Union, but the absolute nullity of the Union. Meagher is its leading genius.

" The Nation" was not strong enough for Mitchell, or Mitchell was too strong for " The Nation," and so he set up " The United Irishman." The United Irishman carries the doctrine of resistance out in its most logical consistency, and to its utmost consequences. It spits upon repeal, it cries for independence ; it calls not only for a national parliament, but for national sovereignty. It laughs at " the golden link of the crown," and holds no terms with O'Connell, to whom this phrase, we believe, is attributed. It scouts Victoria, and mocks Conciliation Hall with as much scorn as it does conciliation. It demands a republic at any cost, and with fierce earnestness it preaches the gospel of the pike. It tells the starving masses of Ireland that they cannot be worse off, and that, with courageous hearts and a strong right hand, they have the power to be better off. It goes even beyond a mere republic. It attacks the present laws and distribution of property, reprobates political economy and its theories, and insists on a reorganization. The editor, John Mitchell, is the son of a Unitarian minister, esteemed by all men who knew him while he lived. He closed a good life, and a long and useful ministry, a few years ago, in the town of Newry, in the north of Ireland. His son, John Mitchell, is undoubtedly a young man of fine talents, ready to do, and dare, and die ; and, if we can judge, prepared for either fortune, — for victory or death, the tribune or the scaffold. His eloquence is brief, bold, fiery, and condensed. If Meagher be the Cicero of the confederates, Mitchell is the Demosthenes of the democrats. The Tablet calls him " the Irish Danton," and so far as strong and burning words, that neither modify nor compromise, are concerned, the designation is not unsuitable ; yet those who know him, speak of him as singularly gentle in personal temper.

It is not our design to enter into either the politics or the purposes of these journals ; but they suggest some remarks on the present condition of Ireland, physical and social.

" Ireland " and " Irish " seem very simple terms, yet do they stand for very complicated things. Ireland, to an American imagination, consists of space extremely limited ; yet, from its earliest history, that space has been most minutely divided. It would not, in mere space, form a leading State of this Union, yet it was once an empire, comprising kingdoms, princedoms, chieftainries. These kingdoms, princedoms, chieftainries had their respective customs, laws, prejudices, with the feuds and factions that spring from such a constitution. Even now, Ireland has her provinces, counties, baronies, in the civil arrangement, with archdioceses, dioceses, parishes, in the ecclesiastical. The English invaders found Ireland a country of manifold partitions, with a people as subdivided as its surface.

"Irish" is a word of most composite signification also. We wonder at the ignorance of writers on this country in their strictures on American character. But surely the ignorance of our own writers on the character of other nations is scarcely less, and much less excusable. We wonder that authors of any intelligence should confound, under one general idea, the reckless men of the West with the orderly men of the East ; the ardent men of the South with the cool men of the North ; the men who hold slaves, with peculiar training as well as peculiar institutions, with other men who have no such training and no such institutions. Yet we are, ourselves, in much grosser error in our popular conception of the Irish. We have, in general, no notion of them but as exiles and drudges. "Irish" means with us a class of human beings, whose women do our house-work, and whose men dig our railroads.

Judging merely by the senses, we are not much to blame, for these are the relations in which, from infancy, we are accustomed to know them. We have indeed heard of Burke, and Grattan, and Curran, with many other great names besides ; we have a sort of persuasion that these were Irishmen ; but when we try practically to consider them as the compatriots of a mud covered laborer in the bed of a canal, the contrast is too violent, and by no force of imagination can we bring such extremes together. We, as a people, are intolerant of ragged garments and empty paunches. We would replace the rags by decent raiment, and we would fill the paunches with wholesome food ; but we have only small respect for those who come to us in tatters, and who rush to us from famine. We are a people who have had no experience in physical tribulation ; and we do not understand the virtues or the vices which such tribulation can produce. We do not know the fearful selfishness which exceeding want may generate ; but neither do we know the blessed charities which it may exhibit, the holy self-denial which it may manifest. As a consequence, the ill-clad and destitute Irishman is repulsive to our habits and to our tastes. We confound ill-clothing and destitution with ignorance and vice, for thus they are associated among ourselves; and that fancy is a rare one which can emancipate itself from the power of habit and the impressions of experience. The crowds that cross the Atlantic to seek a refuge here are, in general, a ragged contrast to our own well covered masses; and, thus rude in external appearance, many find it hard to reach the kindred and immortal humanity which is so coarsely tabernacled. Many of us look only at the outside; we do not enter into the soul. We observe the crushed animal, but we hold no converse with the hidden spirit; we have abundance of pity, but we fail in reverence.

It is a foolish thing to judge of a building by a brick; but the folly is yet greater not to examine even the brick. Irish society is but very partially represented by the portions of it that we have the opportunity of seeing. The structure of Irish society has been very variously and gradually built up, and by materials from a great many quarries. First, there was the old Celtic race; then the Milesian; then the Danes; then the Anglo-Normans and Anglo-Saxons; then the Scottish colonists sent by the first James; then the troopers of Cromwell and the boors of the third William. Now each of these successive invasions deposited a new element of discord, and stratum was laid upon stratum of rebellion and confiscation. Out of rebellion and confiscation have proceeded perpetual strife and hatred. But among the worst results, we must regard that condition of things as the most unfortunate, which transferred the whole soil of the nation to the hands of strangers, and which placed over the people an alien and unsympathizing aristocracy. We have some observations to make on this condition of things as we proceed. The English in the beginning found the Irish broken up among themselves into conflicting factions. This, too, was unhappy. Had it been otherwise, had the Irish been one, had they been concentrated into a national integrity, as the Saxons were when William the Conqueror gained the battle of Hastings, then either the invaded would have repelled the invader, or one would have absorbed or exterminated the other. Neither of these results followed ; and the strange paradox is accordingly exhibited in the universe, of a progressive physical amalgamation of the bone and sinew of Ireland with the bone and sinew of Britain, carrying along with it an unceasing, an undying hatred of its government. It is, therefore, very absurd to speak of the Irish as if they were a single, simple, primitive, unmixed race. The very contrary is the fact. Perhaps there is not a country on the whole earth, so limited in its dimensions, so complicated in its population ; and this, not only in the elements that still continue separate, but also in those that have mingled and coalesced.

It has been common to ascribe the agitations and disorders which so frequently convulse Ireland, to the impatient and turbulent passions of the Celt, to his inherent love of battle and disturbance, to his unruly and rebellious disposition. No position was ever more false than this; not only is it without proof, but against proof. The Celts are not especial rebels; and, indeed, they never have been. The districts in Ireland most troublesome to Britain have always been those which the British colonized; and thus it has been from the days of Strongbow to those of Mitchell. The region in which Cromwell found his hardest task, and that in which he left the most atrocious memory, was that which had its population from English blood. If England has done Ireland wrong, Providence has brought a chastising retribution on her, by means of her own children. The sins of English fathers are not merely visited on their children, but through their children the visitation comes. The most sanguinary page of Cromwell's campaign in Ireland, is that which opens at Drogheda and concludes in Wexford. Likewise in 1798, the counties which earliest entered the conflict, and which longest sustained it, were those wherein the descendants of the British chiefly resided. Wexford fought with desperation, and fought to the last ; and Vinegar Hill, with its broken windmill, remains to this hour a memento of courage and a monument of despair.

Let us now take a rapid survey of the two broad divisions of Irish society. We begin with the aristocracy. And by the aristocracy we mean, principally, the owners of the soil ; we mean, in general, the landlords, and their immediate kindred. Most of those who have fortunes sufficiently large live in England, or on the Continent, deserting at the same time their country and their duties. The greater number have inherited their estates by conquest or confiscation ; and they have never become native to the land that gives them luxury, but that denies life to the wretched men who till it. Accident has made them Irish, and their life is a long regret for being so. They scourge the unhappy nation in which they have had the misfortune to be born, and which has had the still greater misfortune to bear them. The members of this class, who have to stay at home because they are not rich enough to go abroad, constitute the local magistrates, and fill most of the influential local offices. A large majority of the class is utterly bankrupt, insolvent over and over. Most of these men have but the name of property ; for what are called their estates lie under piles of mortgages and incumbrances. Debt has been heaped upon debt, by each generation in its turn, so that it would be as puzzling to a lawyer to discover the original possession, as it would be to a geologist to describe the primitive condition of this planet. Entails, and other artificial contrivances, have long kept estates in families, and held them from the last action of the law on the part of creditors. But even if they could be sold, they would afford only a miserable percentage on the sums for which they have been, time after time, pawned. There is a story of an Irishman who travelled over England with a pig of peculiar sagacity and buoyancy. The pig was lean, lank, and rough; but she had the vigor of a race-horse, and the elasticity of a greyhound. Walls she despised, and gates could not confine her. Her master, each morning, was a little space on his road, when she was after him, and each morning they began a new day most lovingly together. Availing himself of the animal's excellent qualities, the fellow sold her at every stage of his journey, being certain, at each successive sale, that he would have her to sell again. The pig which was thus so often sold was, probably, not honestly come by at first. This elastic animal is no bad representative of landed property in Ireland; we leave it to the imagination of our readers to find out the analogy and to apply it.

Nature has its laws in society, as irrefragable as those it has in matter. Not in one case more than in the other can there be any permanent violation of them. Soon or late, they vindicate themselves. A state of things like that which we have just described cannot last. It must die of its own corruptions, or it must explode, by the force of a pressure that has reached the limit of enduring capacity. The ancestors of Irish landlords bequeathed them broad domains, but with them they bequeathed titles to them that were written and sealed with blood, guarded by a system of legislation that was shocking to humanity. They bequeathed memories of rankling irritation, which the descendants of the injurers were as unable to forget as the descendants of the injured; which the descendants of the injurers were more unwilling to forgive. Wealth that is acquired by violence is seldom spent with wisdom. Economy is as much the offspring of virtue as of labor. We manage that, and that alone, well, which we gain, not simply by toil, but by honest toil. Let no body of men imagine that they can grow rich by conquest. It is not merely a crime to assume such a position, it is a folly, a delusion; it is a blunder. The most dearly purchased treasure is that which is acquired by the sword. The highest price for land or gold is blood. Every nation which has gained either, on such condi-

tions, has perished by them ; and it deserved to perish.
The ancestors of the Irish aristocracy, from the Catholic
Normans to the Puritan Cromwellians, thus obtained
their property ; they left it to their children, adding to
it the penal legacy of prodigal extravagance and profli-
gate habits.

Our description is general. We know that among
the gentry of Ireland there are many and noble exceptions ; and being exceptions, they have our greater admiration. The most common virtues become sublime,
when the opposite vices are all but universal. When
neglect and oppression of the poor spread over a land,
the spots on which they receive some degree of care
and kindness appear as little Edens ; but they are
Edens in a desert. We speak of the Irish gentry as a
class ; and as a class neither their origin nor training,
neither their temper nor circumstances, fit them to con-
ciliate, to foster, or to improve the masses that surround
them. They never had power over the hearts of the
people ; and that power of coercion which they once
possessed, they have not ceased to love, though they
have for ever lost it. We mean, especially, their
monopoly of political influence. Their power as pro-
prietors they yet hold and love ; they do not fail to use
it either, and to use it as badly as ever. Becoming, as
we have seen, deeper in debt with each generation,

one anticipating the income of the other, their tastes and desires have, in the same order, been growing more costly. They may have become more refined, but they also have become more expensive. The deadly competition for land in Ireland enables them to raise rents to the highest sum that human labor can produce, and to press down living to the lowest condition that human nature can endure. The tenant is cast upon the ragged soil, to tear from its bosom payment for his master, and starvation for himself. In the latter he always succeeds; and when he fails in the former, the master, by means of arrears, holds in his hands the power to expel him. The owner spends no capital on the soil; he builds no houses or offices; he furnishes no implements; he pursues no experiments in agriculture; he does not instruct the tenant, either by theory or example; and when some year worse than others leaves the tenant at his mercy, the mercy that many a landlord shows is to turn him off, with neither allowance nor compensation for such improvements as he has struggled in his poverty to make.

We fancy some of our readers complaining about the everlasting historical references, to account for the state of Ireland. Why, we conceive them saying, why this reiteration of matters that are gone to the grave of centuries, to explain what our eyes see and our ears hear ? But they are not gone to the grave of centuries; they were but sown in the living soil of centuries, and now they are ripened into a heavy harvest of a most black and bitter crop. We cannot understand present events without understanding their historical connection, and least of all can we understand those of Ireland; and to us, especially, young among the nations, the example of our elders is important. As it is, the lesson that history teaches does not seem entirely needless to us. Recent as is our independent existence, we have gone far in the pathway of the Old World, and, instead of looking to it as a beacon, we seem rather to follow it as a star. It is more our model than our warning; we study the lesson the wrong way; and it is well if we do not in that wrong way outrun the instruction. We, too, have our oppressions and our injustice. Under the very shadow of our Capitol, while the welkin rings with gratulations which are to stir with joy the heart of France, a mob gathers to crush free thought, — thought dedicated to the widest liberty and to the highest humanity; nay, at the very time that shouts of execration were sent across the broad Atlantic, to blast a fallen monarch in his exile, tyrants with hearts harder than the hearts of tigers were tearing off their human brothers and sisters from the region of their native affections, consigning them to a slavery, compared with which their former slavery seemed freedom, dead to their agony of spirit, chaining them with iron, that did not gall half so terribly as the iron that had entered into their soul; and all because, prompted by instincts which God and nature had implanted, they sought that freedom for which God and nature had designed them. What a mockery is this! What right have such men to hoot at Louis Philippe, contrasted with whom Louis Philippe is an angel of light? What title have such men to vociferate acclamations for liberty? Liberty is but insulted by their praise. We, too, seem in a fair way to enthrone the soldier, and to idolize the sword; to give strength the place of virtue, and victory the place of right. But let us not be deceived. God is no more mocked by nations with impunity than by individuals; and nations, as well as individuals, will reap according to what they sow. We may despise the lesson of history, but we cannot reverse its law; and this law is made evident in the records of all ages. Wrong and right make no account of time, they are certain and eternal; their consequences may not be instantly seen, but they are not lost; nay, they do not even linger.

There is but one step from the aristocracy to the peasantry in Ireland, and that step is over a fearful precipice into an abyss of indescribable, of unimaginable desolation. There are but few intermediate grades to break the view, or to soften the contrast; it is a yawning gulf, exposed in all its horrors, from which the gazer shrinks back affrighted, with a reeling head and with quivering nerves. Yet must we, however loath, ask our readers to lean with us for a moment over it.

The physical state of the Irish peasantry did not, in past times, seem capable of being lower than it was. Even then, it was the lowest which any region of the civilized world could present. Their dwellings were hovels; their clothing, rags; and their food, an almost unseasoned root. But all this was paradise to what their state has been since, — to what it is now. The very root which was so despised, we have come to regard almost with reverence; and when we see how, by the withering of this single root, hundreds of thousands of human beings withered along with it, we can understand how the heathen Egyptians bowed down to leeks in worship. The grave of the potato seed was the grave of men, women, and children; but the potato died knowing not its own existence, while the men, women, and children that perished with it expired in ghastly and consuming torture, with blank despair of this inhospitable world; yet, thank God! not untrustful of a better. Far off though it was, we heard the low moaning of that despair, for at the extremities of earth the heart of man can feel the pantings of another heart that suffers, and, even where it cannot give relief, it fails not to give pity.

Who can faintly picture what even one family must have endured in such circumstances? Think of them turning their weary eyes around on the arid fields, and up to the sky, that seemed to grow sickly to them from hour to hour; awaking in the morning, without a morsel to greet them; watching through the day, counting minute after minute, awaiting the possible relief that never came, or that came too late; clasping each other on the filthy straw, or bare cold floor, through the miserable night; sleeping to dream of feasting, awaking to die of famine. And yet we have not reached the worst part of the case. The most fatal pain lies here, not in the appetites, but in the affections. Look at the emaciated father, who comes in after vain search all day for food, and has nothing to offer his wife and little ones but a meal of unwholesome herbs, picked out of the ditches; look at him when he can find even these no longer, when competition has consumed them. Has it entered into the heart to conceive of his affliction? Yet is that of the wife and mother even greater, who beholds the manly form bent and wasted, of him that had been once her strength and her guide ; who beholds her chickens clustering about her, opening their craving mouths for food, and drooping as they get none. This picture is pale to what the reality must have been ; and of such realities there was no small number. It is to be feared that they have not yet passed ; nay, it is to be feared that some are now passing.

The Irish peasant in former days had a hut, such as it was ; but in these days his master hunts him out of it, as if he were a rat, and the land refuses him a hole for shelter. The workhouse is full ; the jail would be relief, and he breaks the law for refuge in a prison ; but by and by crime itself will be as fruitless as charity, and the prisons will not bear the throngs that seek them. In former days the Irish peasant sat down to his potatoes, and while they laughed in his face, his partner and his offspring laughed around him. His cabin was of mud, covered with sods or straw ; but it gave him a home, and, in general, love and peace abode in it. Nor was hospitality absent. No poor-laws existed, yet were beggars fed; no workhouses were in being, yet were beggars lodged ; the pauper had his seat at the peasant's meal, he had his covering under the peasant's roof.

If his condition even then was physically still below that of the Russian serf or the negro slave, what shall

we say of his present condition? The Russian is a
filthy creature in all his habits; but his filth coexists
with comfort and abundance. His filth is of his own
creation, and he remains filthy because he chooses to
do so. His dwelling is rude, but it is warm; his food
is coarse, but it is plentiful. He is in no fear that any
landlord will turn him out, for he has the right to continue where he toils, and to die where he was born. If
he must serve the emperor when the emperor commands, he knows what his lot is, and he does not
complain of it. In general, he glories in it; for to be
changed from being a serf into a soldier is to rise in his
own esteem. Without overlooking the degradation of
humanity and the sorrow which slavery inflicts upon
the negro, in the mere matter of bodily well-being,
there is no comparison between his state and that of
the Irish peasant. It is the interest of his master that
he shall have at least so much care as shall render him
a saleable article or a profitable laborer. His master is
induced to give him a healthy youth, and he is bound
to provide for him in age; it is his interest even that he
shall enjoy mental quiet and contentment, for the more
cheerful he is, the more useful. No doubt he is often
subjected to cruelty; but even to the slave Christianity
is a protection, for it infuses a sentiment into the moral
heart, and creates a power of social opinion, which is

stronger than law, stronger than tyranny ; and these, if they do not break the yoke, alleviate bondage. Unlike the Russian serf, the Irish peasant's home is uncertain, and it is his master's desire not to keep him, but to cast him off; and while all the power is on one side, there is no acknowledged claim on the other. Unlike the negro slave, the Irish peasant has no hold on the interest of his lord, as he certainly has no hold on his affections. He has no public opinion, in the class to which his lord belongs, to shield him from oppression, and the sympathy which he has among his own is such as tempts him often to revenge himself by methods always to be lamented. He may stand in manhood or sink in age, there is none but God on whom he can cast the burden of his care ; for among men, those who feel for him and with him are as helpless as himself.

We have already stated a sad case, but we know from every week's report, that, at present, other terrible elements are at work. The potato withered last year ; this year the pike is forged and whetted. Fierce and dark passions are boiling in the breasts of men, and threaten to burst out in the tempest of civil, bloody strife, with all its hatreds and terrors. Despair has ceased to be quiescent ; it has started up in wildness from its lair, and shakes its Gorgon locks in deadly anger; it has ceased to wail, it thunders; and if it does not strike, it grasps its weapon.

It were vain to enter specially into causes which have produced effects, such as these we have been describing. Whatever causes we might assign, remote or proximate, there is still an actuality before us of a most appalling character, — a whole people starving amidst fertility, and arising in madness to look for hope in the face of death. Before this spectacle, abstract questions lose all their interest; our gaze is fascinated by the misery which is before us, which stares on us with horrid eye, and from which we cannot turn away, though we look on it with trembling. The plain, open wretchedness is there; but it so appalls us, that we are unable to inquire or to discuss how it came to be there; and the babble of discussion on hypotheses to account for hunger and revolt, by men who feed amply and feed at ease, is as offensive to our taste as the affliction itself is painful to our feelings. Whatever series of causes has issued in the effects which we contemplate, we see evidently and with alarm that it cannot stop, that it is not exhausted in these effects. We hope and trust that all these irritating elements may be lost in peaceful amelioration.

The British power has many and grave crimes to answer for; but we should lament with no common lamentation the wound that civilization must receive, not merely in the disruption of the British empire, but in any severe shock to it. The shower of lava that buries a single city, the earthquake that shakes one to pieces, history notes down in words of pathos and sadness that move the heart for ever. But the disorder which should tear to atoms, laws, letters, culture, customs, — which should crumble to dust beautiful structures of public and private taste, — which should reduce to chaos arts of fancy and utility, — all of which it has taken centuries to rear, — would be a calamity to be compared, not with a shower of lava, a torrent, a hurricane, an earthquake, but with a deluge which should come down from the black wrath of heaven, and bury in its flood, not millions only, but the works of millions also for a thousand years. Yet we feel that in the British islands affairs cannot continue as they are. In no part of them are the people contented; in Ireland they are mad. They are in the extremity of wretchedness; it is no wonder they should be in the extremity of desperation. The Irish people are starving, and yet the Irish soil is not barren. With all the ill treatment which it has to bear, it yet continues rich; the clouds pour down fatness and the earth gives forth abundance, yet multitudes do not so much live as wither. The soil is vital, while the people die.

It seemed a mystery to the inhabitants of this country how thousands should expire of hunger at a time when provisions were sent away from every port ; and why, while the war-ship went in with charity, the merchant-ship should go out for gain, both freighted with the staff of life. The mystery is easily explained. The manufacture and the commerce of Ireland consist generally in the production of food and its exportation. The manufacturers are the tillers of the soil, who give in their labor all the capital, and pay high rents besides for that on which they toil. The landlords are the owners of the soil, who expend no capital, and who take even more than the profit. The land cannot support these two classes, as they are at present related. The landlord must have state and luxury, not expending time or labor or money, though the tenant, spending time and labor and money, has not subsistence. The best of the produce, animal and vegetable, is exported to meet the landlord's demands ; the worst is retained to supply the cultivator's wants. The cultivator must pay or quit. He sells his wheat, his oats, his stock, to pay ; he reserves the potato, on which to exist. The potato fails ; the cultivator becomes a pauper or a corpse. But all are not thus at once, and so, while wheat is going out from Cork from some to pay the landlord, maize is coming in for alms to others, who have already paid him. A man will feed his pig with potatoes, but he may never feed himself with pig. The man feeds the pig but to sell it, and he sells it to pay one who had never had trouble in rearing it. Rent not only takes the surplus production of the tiller's labor, but constantly anticipates even more than the whole. It may, then, easily be seen how the mass of a plentiful general productiveness may be going out from a country, while the mass of its producers are running to the workhouse or famishing in their cabins.

We write practically and prosaically. We should more delight ourselves, in writing upon Ireland, to write poetically; for Ireland has much, indeed, to stir the spirit of poetry. Ireland is a land of poetry. The power of the Past there over every imagination renders it a land of romance. The past is yet an actuality in Ireland; in all the other parts of the British islands it is a song. The tragedy of Flodden Field moves a Scotchman's feelings, but it does not disturb his business; the battle of Bannockburn calls up his enthusiasm, but, though it keeps him late at the bottle, it never keeps him late from the counting-house. The imprisonment of the poet-king Jamie softens his affections, but it leaves his judgment perfectly clear on bills of exchange and the price of stocks. Even the battle of Culloden is gone long ago to the calm impartiality of things that were. The Welshmen take English money without remorse, and say not a word about the assassin, King Edward, and the murder of their bards. Even the English themselves have but faint remembrance of the heptarchy, the revolt of the barons, the wars of the roses, the death of the first Charles, and the abdication of the second James. But events do not pass so rapidly in Ireland. Ireland is a country of tradition, of meditation, and of great idealism. It has much of the Eastern feeling of passion added to fancy, with continuity of habit, as in the East, connected with both passion and fancy. Monuments of war, of princedom, and religion cover the surface of the land. The meanest man lingers under the shadow of piles which tell him that his fathers were not slaves. He toils in the field or he walks on the highways with structures before him that have stood the storms of time, through which the wind echoes with the voice of centuries, and that voice is to his heart the voice of soldiers, of scholars, and of saints. We would pen no chilling word respecting the impulse of nationality that now seems astir in Ireland. We honor every where the spirit of nationality. We honor the glorious heroism which, for an idea and a conviction, if it cannot do, can always dare and die.

Much there is in Ireland that we most dearly love. We love its music, sweet and sad, and low and lonely ;

it comes with a pathos, a melancholy, a melody, on the pulses of the heart, that no other music breathes, and while it grieves, it soothes. It seems to flow with long complaint over the course of ages, or to grasp with broken sobs through the ruins and fragments of historic thought. We are glad with the humor of Ireland, so buoyant and yet so tender, quaint with smiles, quivering with sentiment, pursing up the lips while it bedews the eyelids. We admire the bravery of Ireland, which may have been broken, but never has been bent, — which has often been unfortunate, but which never has been craven. We have much affection for the Irish character. We give unfeigned praise to that purity of feeling which surrounds Irish women in the humblest class, and amidst the coarsest occupations, with an atmosphere of sanctity. We acknowledge with heartfelt satisfaction that kindred love in the Irish poor, that no distance can weaken, and that no time can chill. We feel satisfied with our humanity, when we see the lowly servant girl calling for her wages, or drawing on the savings' bank for funds, to take tears from the eyes of a widowed mother in Connaught, or fears from the soul of an aged father in Munster. We behold a radiance of grandeur around the head of the railroad laborer, as he bounds, three thousand miles away, at the sound of repeal, at the name of O'Connell, and

yet more as his hand shakes, as he takes a letter from the
post-office, which, rude as it may be in superscription,
is a messenger from the cot in which his childhood lay,
is an angel from the fields, the hills, the streams, the
mountains, and the moors wherein his boyhood sported.
We remember with many memories of delight, too,
the beauties of Ireland's scenery. We recollect the
fields that are ever green ; the hills that bloom to the
summit ; the streamlets that in sweetness seem to sing
her legends ; the valleys where the fairies play ; the
voices among her glens, that sound from her winds as
with the spirits of her bards ; the shadows of her ruins
at moonlight, that in pale and melancholy splendor
appear like the ghosts of her ancient heroes.   We
would, could we choose our theme, rather linger on the
beautiful songs of Moore than on the prosecutions of
Meagher or of Mitchell ; and if in this paper we have
dwelt more upon the physical and social wants of Ireland than on her higher and more ideal qualities, it is
because the immediate pressure of present events has
left us neither soul nor strength to do otherwise.

But what is to come out of this pressure ? We ask
the question with fear and doubt. Is Ireland to come
in conflict with England ?   We cannot always trust
rumor, but rumor is at present dark and ominous. The
event, we hope, may not come ; but the very sound of

it is fearful. War, in any way, is a monstrous calamity ; but civil war is a calamity that transcends
imagination. War between England and Ireland would
be a civil war, — there is no disguising it, — and a
civil war of the worst description. We ask not which
party would be right, but still we reiterate that this
would be among the greatest of calamities. We do
not inquire what title England has to govern Ireland,
but we do ask what means Ireland has to combat
England.

We think that in revolutions, as in all human movements, there are certain ethical conditions, as well as
prudential ones, which true men and wise will always
respect. War has its morals as well as peace. Moreover, as war is of all controversies the most afflicting,
as it is that which most involves innocent persons who
have had no part in bringing it about, who yet may
suffer the worst of its consequences, it should be the
last, as it should be the most solemn, of human re-
solves. And if war is not to be sustained by civilized
measures, if there is no guaranty that humanity even
in its last strife shall be respected, to originate it is to
assume a terrible responsibility. If citizen is to butcher
citizen, if the revolters are to exterminate the loyal,
and the loyal to show no mercy to the revolters, if one
has no power to compel the other even to military

moderation, alas, alas for him who sets on the strife ! Revolution may be an accident ; but if it be a calculation, it should be a very sober calculation ; at best, it should be a very sad one. The simple fact, that a man thinks little of his own life, gives him no title to our respect ; for the lowest of the human family have been found in this predicament. We have seen culprits at the bar stand up to receive the sentence of death, and even among the basest we have noticed those who listened to the sentence perfectly calm, and the most unmoved. When the lives of others are concerned, the man who cares nothing for his own often the longest hesitates. With the most determined conviction of the right, it is the thing most sorrowful beneath the stars to have brothers of the same soil making a red sea with the life-streams of each other's hearts, in which, with curses and detestation, both sink in despair together.

Then, in cases that involve vast consequences both to masses and to individuals, the prudential does, in the highest sense, become ethical ; so that what is extremely dangerous is extremely wrong. What are the means and resources of war, at present, in the war-party of Ireland against England ? This is not an unwise question, for He who was best and wisest has said, " What king, going to make war against another king, sitteth not down first and consulteth whether he be able with tèn thousand to meet him that cometh against him with twenty thousand ? " They who would by force deliberately revolutionize, must, if true, thoroughly ponder this question, and in the great court of conscience they must not only ponder, but decide. A physical struggle with England, as a mere physical struggle, would to a thoughtful man just now present a serious case within this court, and outside of it the consequences would be most solemn. England is at peace. England is, on the whole, prudent as to her colonies and her foreign relations. England has fleets and armies compactly organized and thoroughly disciplined. England impels all the organic machinery of the law and of power. Within Ireland she has a numerous party, and the most consummate statesmanship, which would oppose Irish nationality ; the most veteran soldiership, which would fight against Irish independence, would be of Irish production. The composite nature of the British empire, which might appear to be a weakness, is in reality a principle of strength. And this, by a revolutionary thinker, should be considered in relation to the *matériel* of the British army.

There is no army in the world in which the soldier is so separated from the citizen as in the British.

There is no army in the world, which, from its compounded character, the government can better wield. A man from the north of Scotland may stand in the ranks beside a man from the south of England; both may be opposed to an Irish insurgent, — be cordially willing to shoot him, and, if cause demanded, to shoot each other. The army is so mixed, from localities, religions, prejudices, that it has no unity of spiritual sentiment or of social purpose; it fears not to rush against the deadliest resistance, but it would not dare to disobey the most faintly whispered command. England can use this gigantic instrument. It is for those who would lead Ireland into war to think what Ireland can bring against it. She has a tremendous artillery, both on the land and on the sea. Nor is her strength in force alone. She has on her side the fears of the timid, and the hopes of the aspiring; the distinction that allures the ambitious, and the riches that bribe the sordid.

If, however, there be ethical and prudential considerations to be taken into view on the side of resistance, there are those of infinitely more solemn obligation on the side of authority. On the moral side of the question, it is for rulers to inquire whether the madness and misery of the people are not traceable to the neglect and misusage of the people. It is for rulers to ask

themselves whether the millions have had justice done
even to their bodies.   Have men had leave to toil, and
when they have had that melancholy leave, have they
had by it the means to live?   In what way have the
vanity or indulgences of the few interfered with the
industry and comforts of the many?   And when the
many at last make their sufferings felt, is complaint to
be silenced by force?   If in the end the blood of
thousands flow, upon whose head must that blood be
charged?   The conduct of members in the British
House of Commons, on the evening of the day of the
Chartist meeting, strikes us with a painful surprise.
Bodies of gaunt men gathered within view of the metropolis, — a cloud of silent but of potent passions,
that hovered on its margin with dread foreboding.
The metropolis itself was one vast garrison.   Men
were silent, women feared ; and neither breathed
freely till the assurance came, with night, that danger
had disappeared.   On the other side of the Channel,
resistance was openly and fearlessly preached, and it
was not alone preached, but prepared for.   On that
solemn night, — a night one might suppose in which
the most reckless would be serious, when, if men stood
in England on solid ground, the rest of Europe was
heaving with a moral earthquake, — on that night, the
assembled Commons of the British empire met the

complaints of infuriated masses with peals of con-
temptuous laughter. This was assuredly as far from
the grave decency which they owed to the occasion, as
it was from the dignity of senators and the wisdom of
statesmen. When heathen Nineveh was threatened,
her rulers decreed penance in sackcloth and ashes;
when Christian London was threatened, her legislators
laughed. Such laughter sounds more like the rebound
of cowardice freed from danger, than the levity of
tranquil courage; the laughter, not of self-possession,
but of trepidation. If thoughtless, it was folly, and if
intentional, it was worse. Are property, privilege, and
power to have all attention and respect, while want and
labor are for mockery and scorn? Such conduct implies neither magnanimity nor good sense.

It is for rulers to ask themselves whether the millions
have had justice done to their minds. Ireland has had
for centuries a church of monstrous inutility and enormous wealth forced on her, against her creed and her
consent, with revenues that would have instructed all
her people, and done much to feed her poor. England
lavishes funds with imperial prodigality over the whole
earth, as well as within her own borders, but is penu-
rious with miser meanness in the support of popular
instruction. The cost of Prince Albert's stables would
educate a province. The cost of the queen's nursery

would educate a kingdom.   How are incongruities like
this, — and this is but one of a legion, — to be endured
in the nineteenth century, when the human mind has
awakened to its rights and to its power, when human
energies assume a might with which they never acted
before ?   The most ragged Chartist is a man, as well as
the best clad lord ; and take the clothes away, God and
nature have not placed any immeasurable distance between them, after all.   Of the two, the Chartist may
be the better man, and the Chartist is beginning to feel
this.   If the Chartist owes submission to the laws of
his country, his country owes obligations to him ; and
all moralists concede that there is a boundary beyond
which submission ceases to be a virtue.   It is the duty
of wise and good rulers never to let that boundary be
reached.   If authority demands obedience, authority
should be so used that the obedience may be willing as
well as rational.   This is not only true humanity ; it is
good policy.

Thus expediency teaches the same lesson to rulers
as morality.   The victory over the Chartists, notwithstanding the boastings of the middle classes and the
nobles, was a doleful victory.   If it showed the strength
of government, it equally displayed its danger.   Masses
made the commencement of a demonstration, which
may be only the beginning of an end.   The Chartists

hand, the hand of a soldier. Still war, itself, originate how it may, and issue how it will, is, in its immediate action, the saddest manifestation of humanity.
War, if extended, and long continued, oppresses or
destroys industry, lessens comforts, paralyzes education, debases morals, undermines and corrupts religion. The highest liberty is in harmony with the
highest laws. But war, for the time, suspends all
the highest laws; war gives force the place of
right, and force must hold that place, while war goes
on; war gives force the place of the Gospel, and it
reverses nearly every charity which the Gospel enjoins.
The injunction of the Gospel is to do good to an enemy;
but that of war is to do him injury, and all the injury
that is possible. Nay, the ethics of war maintain that
this is the most humane, because the more terrrible the
evil, the sooner its conclusion. Nor is it to the direct
and fighting foe that the injury is done, but to the innocent who are associated with him; not to the strong
man only, who stands against his opponent, face to
face, and foot to foot, but to the woman sitting by the
cradle, and to the guileless child that sleeps in it.
War, bloody, cruel, and ruthless, lets fly unheeding its
missiles of destruction, cares not where the ball shall
kill, or where the bomb shall burst; and, whether they
tear to fragments the sunny boy, that last night was

dreaming of his sports, or mangle the beautiful girl who was enchantment in her home, it is still the same in its blind atrocity. Without imagination, without sensibility, it goes forth to butchery; and when it has made a slaughter-house of some fair spot, rent to pieces thousands of human bodies, temples of the holy ghost, it yells forth its triumph for a work in which we might suppose that only devils would rejoice; it puts forth its hallelujah amidst such agonies and such crimes, that we might conceive that only hell would give it an amen! The fruits of the Gospel are love, forbearance, meekness, purity, joy; those of war are hatred, vengeance, lust, carnage, and misery.

The best progress coincides with the best civilization; the best progress does not consist in accumulation of wealth. That nation in the world which had the earliest revelation of holy things, and which was, for centuries, the treasury of divine ideas, was, upon the whole, a poor nation. That nation, too, which has been of all nations, the most perfect in human development, was never rich; that nation, which embodied all conceptions of the beautiful, and so transcendently embodied them, that mankind have done nothing ever since, but admire them, and despair; that nation, which carried intellect to the limits of thought, and exhausted all philosophies; that nation, which gave to language enchanting harmony, and enriched it in epic, lyric, drama, history, eloquence, with a literature that is unrivalled and immortal; that nation, which gave to virtue, examples of heroic worth which shame the selfishness of every age, and to patriotism, names so illustrious and inspiring, as still to set the coldest blood on fire; that nation was scattered among crags in the Mediterranean, and had, probably, never so much wealth as some mercantile associations of our own day.

But, lacking, as that nation was, in gold and silver, it has bestowed imperishable wealth on all succeeding generations; it has furnished to them all the types of their mental existence, all the ideals of their artistic aspirations; it has entwined itself with all the fibres of civilized life, animates its movements, and shapes its forms. It is often when wealth accumulates, that men decay. The decline of Rome began when it was gorged with the riches of the provinces. The downfall of Spain may be dated from the foundation of its empire in the west. It is well if empire in the east does not work the same ruin for England. One thing is plain, for it is before our eyes, that England, at the present day, is at once a miracle of wealth, and a miracle of wretchedness; that her treasures surpass all that the world has ever seen, and so does the suffering of her millions. The lesson is true and terrible.

The best progress is not evinced by a rapidly advancing population. Supposing even that people have both room and plenty, still, for the security of national happiness and national development, character is infinitely more important than numbers. Without character, without the guidance of morals and reason, they are, after all, so much muscle, appetite, and passion. With the utmost scope, and the most abundant subsistence, it strikes me that there is something in such a state of things which is fearful and tremendous. Trust nothing to mere brute man, for the very element of reason, which nothing can wholly destroy, when not united to his nobler aspirations, gives fiercer vigor to his baser desires. He is not, therefore, a mere animal in his grossest propensities; he is something more dangerous. Such propensities in the animal are bounded, in him they are unlimited. And slavery, if we could reduce multitudes to it, would deepen the risk, instead of removing it. When we hold increasing masses of men in bondage, the ultimate risk increases with the masses.

No outward pressure can always keep down the growth of human energy; and the more you enfeeble the divine part of men's nature, the more you invigorate the bestial. Contrive as we may, humanity will hold its power; shear its locks as we please, they will grow again; blind the eyes of its soul as we can, it becomes only the more ruthless in the darkness of its strength, and the hour which finds us in ease and pleasure, may be the one in which it will snap asunder the manacles with which we have bound it; then laying its emancipated hands on the pillars of the social temple, shake to pieces, in madness and despair, the contrivance of wisdom and the labor of ages. The birth of every human being, then, brings to society an incalculable responsibility; a responsibility, which society can alone fulfil, by receiving it as human; by treating it as human, by rendering it, to the degree that it is possible, fit to enjoy a human existence, and to complete, here at least, a human destiny. Thus, and thus alone, is the growth of society a growth of promise.

Nor does the true progress, or true greatness of a nation consist in extent of territory, even though multitudes be added to space. If space and men rendered a nation great, then would Russia, with its hordes of savage serfs, be incomparably the greatest nation in Europe. If multitudes and space together rendered a nation great, then China, with its centuries of monotony, and its millions of machines, is the greatest nation in the world. If territory and population, of themselves, constitute national greatness, then was the Greece of Leonidas less glorious than the Greece of Alexander, and the Rome of Nero more exalted than the Rome of Regulus. But this is not so. No nation advances towards greatness, or in greatness, by the number of its inhabitants or the extension of its sway. This is equally within the power of the most barbarous as of the most refined. Nay, the advantage is on the side of barbarism, as barbarism has the least obstruction from social relations, or from moral restraint. Money, miles, millions, do not render a nation great, not one alone, or all of them together. A nation may have them in united force, and have nothing besides which the world can admire, or which the world will remember. Not even by science, art, and literature does a nation merit to be called great. Even these must have moral inspiration, or they are poor, mean and lifeless. It is only as they are significant of spiritual worth, that they elevate a man, that they elevate society. A nation is, therefore, great only, as it originates great ideas, as it nourishes great sentiments; as it trains great characters; as it venerates and follows great examples; as it is loyal to great principles; as it coördinates power with justice, and as it identifies majesty with goodness.

What more is Liberty worth? Liberty is worth whatever country is worth. It is by liberty that a man

has a country ; it is by liberty he has rights; it is by
rights that he has obligations ; it is by rights and
obligations that his life is that of a citizen, and that
of a patriot. The idea of country is a social idea,
is a moral idea ; and the tie that binds one to his
nation is not sensual, but spiritual. Mere space does
not constitute country ; it is not a boundary that lays
claim upon the soul, that fastens on the heart. Mere
physical support establishes no title to allegiance ; it can
awaken no civic feelings nor impose any civic duty.
I owe the soil nothing for my simple birth ; I owe the
soil nothing in which I own nothing ; I owe the soil
nothing in which I am owned ; and whether, as in a
despotism, I am one of the whole population thus cir-
cumstanced, or, in other conditions, one only of a portion, the principle is the same.

Between these two states, there is, however, a
material difference in practice ; for where slavery is
universal, it cannot be so complete as where it reaches
only a class ; neither is the individual so degraded,
where all stand with him on a common level. I owe
the soil nothing which endures me only for my toil,
and, in return, gives me but feeding and a grave. That
is my country, on whose surface I am a man ; within
whose embrace, I am secured in all the privileges of a
man ; under the majesty of whose laws, I can put forth

the best energies of a man. That is my country, in whose institutions my existence is respected, and in whose greatness I have my portion. It is not my country, because it has the accident of my existence; because it gives me permission to live, but strips me of every power, except the power to die. A slave, therefore, can have no patriotism; and the more he is above his condition, the farther will he be removed from such an emotion; the more there is in him of the man, and the less there is in him of the slave, the less he can love the nation where he can presume to no manhood, and the more he must hate the institutions that fasten him to bondage.

On a level with his condition he can have affectionate instincts, but no moral reason; on a level with his condition, he may be a grateful animal, but not an enlightened intelligence; he may be a pet, he cannot be a patriot. I speak not here of the patriotism of sentiment, of principle, but of the simplest instinct. The savage, in his uncouth freedom, claims ownership in the forest and the plain; he is the citizen of unappropriated nature, and with a wild affection loves the space over which he roams; he is a patriot of the desert. The clansman walks a lord upon the mountains; he bounds elastic on the heather; he gives himself, it is true, to his leader without reserve, but with that leader he claims a kindred, and has his claim allowed. Even the serf, though he labors for the enrichment of another, has a prescriptive association with the land on which he toils ; he has some security for family and a home ; where he was born, he will work, and where he spent his youth, he will spend his age. Degraded as his situation is, it is not without motives to courage and even to heroism ; rising above his immediate circumstances, he has ideals beyond them to give him dignity. If he is the bondsman of his lord, he is the child — so he deems himself — of the emperor ; if each claims an ownership to his services, his spirit can have freedom in the church, which comprehends them all. Of the bravery with which such men could fight, we need not call Napoleon from his grave to testify ; it is written on the most tragic pages of his story. The slave has not the scope of the savage, the kindred of the clansman, or the fixedness of the serf. I allude to the domestic slave.

Political slavery may inflict crushing miseries ; domestic slavery may co-exist with many comforts ; but political slavery admits something to individual humanity, and is not inconsistent with the most intense and stubborn nationality. Domestic slavery assumes for its basis the denial of individual humanity, and, in connection with it, nationality is an utter impossibility.

Domestic slavery is the final limit of subjection and of power; beyond this it is impossible to advance them, in fact, or in conception. The domestic slave is a thing, a chattel; unconditional property; a living anomaly; a creature without a law, that may yet be punished; a creature without a will, that may yet be accountable. He is in the nation, but in no sense of it. He has no interest in the wealth by which it is enriched; he has no part in the laws by which it is governed; he has no dawnings from the genius by which it is enlightened; he has no enjoyment from the arts by which it is adorned; he has no connection with the power by which it is sustained; he has no pride in the glory by which it is exalted; he has no relationship with the history or names, by which its fame has been established. Moral being he has scarcely any, and from religion itself, the slightest monitions, the most dim revealings. A slave can have no patriotism. He cannot know the meaning of the word. He has nothing that inspires the feeling; he has nothing that explains the term. In any sacred, any consecrated sense, a slave can be neither husband nor wife, but producers; neither parent nor child, but offspring; neither brother nor sister. The only legal, the only recognized relationship which the condition of a slave implies, is that of property, that of ownership. A slave cannot be a patriot, he has no country; a slave cannot be a patriot, he has no home.

Here, therefore, I may further add, that liberty is worth whatever life is worth; and if so, as the opposite of partial and political subjection, how much more as the contrast of entire and personal subjection.

That man has a poor and craven disposition, who finds nothing better in life than the replenishment of its sensations, the satisfaction of its appetites. Life is to a man, as man, more than mere animal existence, and its good more than mere physical health. It is in an especial sense, reason, conscience, will, imagination, affection; and its higher good, all that elevates these, exercises, purifies and expands them. Let these be hindered from coming forth, or let them not dare to show themselves, and I am deprived of a human life, or I am forbidden to enjoy one. Liberty, and liberty alone, gives me all for which existence is greatly valuable; mind, speech, education, law, security, social station, and social claims; kindred, home, country. Make me but once the property of another; let me live by his will and for his advantage; let me have nothing that in result I can call mine; let him own my muscle and its toil; let him own my intellect and its skill; let my home and all that it contains be at his disposal; then every evil which Heaven can rain down upon me, with which earth can scourge me, is in comparison a trivial visitation. All after this, that men esteem as good, has lost its savor. Feed me with dainties, clothe me with splendor, let me live in the midst of grandeur, look not on me but with smiles, speak not to me but in praise; but let me be enslaved, my days will be sad, my nights will be heavy, my imprisoned spirit will find no pleasure in them; it will watch anxiously for the hour, as the sick look for the morning, when the weary go to rest, and the servant is free from his master. Give me hardship, pain, toil; but with them give me liberty, and I shall not complain; but sooner, a thousand times, than I should wear the garment of a slave, let me be stiff in the shroud of a freeman.

So native is this desire to the heart of man, that liberty is a dream which gilds the sleep of the most besotted slave; it rises as a beautiful vision in the nightly silence of his lonely hut; it comes to him as a sad, fond hope in the intervals of toil, and for a moment it cheats him with the delusions of a man. The faintest chance of liberty is often sufficient to charm him through every danger; to sustain him through thousands of miles unknown; to carry him across swamp and desert, and forest; to support him under cold and hunger, nakedness and fatigue; to quell in his bosom the fear of the hound and the fear of the rifle ; sufficient to cheer him along, all unaided and alone, with no guide outside him but the northern star, and no prompting from within but an indomitable instinct.

Some may say, that liberty is nothing but a sound, and slavery nothing but a name ; yet, assuredly, that sound must have a mighty power, which in every age could stir men to enthusiasm, that never has died out ; which in every age could quicken those emotions that men have always esteemed generous and heroic. I cannot even conceive, how any man can see another, however low, struggling to be free, without feeling with him, without desiring from the bottom of his heart, God-speed, without admiring his effort, without pitying him in failure, without applauding him in success. And if slavery is indeed only a name, it must be one that carries along with it a terrible delusion ; since no man can be found, who ever knew liberty in its very worst condition, who would volunteer to be a slave. Men go dauntlessly to the field red with slaughter ; they shrink not from the stark bodies of their comrades ; without a tremor they rush to the cannon's mouth that vomits out destruction ; but not one can you discover, who would knowingly enter into slavery. Despised and trampled down, as the wretched often are in communities deemed free, they have ever regarded slavery as still a lower deep. Men have known life in its worst calamities, but they have never, in their wildest fancies, thought on slavery for relief. Men have become sick of existence, and poverty has driven many to despair; numbers have rid themselves of life, but not one has ever sold it. It was then no burst of enthusiasm, it was no exaggeration of rhetoric, it was deliberate conviction, it was well-considered resolve, it was wise, it was sober choice, which prompted the orator to exclaim, " Give me liberty, or give me death ! "

Nay, liberty is not only worth all that life is worth, it is worth all that the soul is worth. All that belongs truly to the soul, belongs to its freedom; all that comes out truly from the soul, comes out from its freedom. Thought, belief, affection, worship, these belong to the soul, and they are free; they are beyond the reach of purchase; they are beyond the reach of power. Word, deed, suffering; these are great as they come out from the soul, as they come out from its freedom. In every word, in every deed, in every suffering, that is greatest, wherein there is the spirit of a free soul. What word of man, of highest and of boldest import, that does not come out fearlessly from the soul, and go forth unchained, upon the air of liberty ? Thus it is, that the prophet issues from out his wilderness, seeking the presence of people and of kings, to give them his message from above, and to pour forth the burden of his awful inspiration. Thus it is, that the true orator, secular or sacred, stands before his fellows with unfettered intellect, with courageous heart, to speak what the occasion requires, what honesty impels. His position may have danger, but his thought will not admit constraint; his position may be that of Paul in the presence of Felix; but though bonds were on the hands of Paul, his spirit was unchained. It may be that of Emmett in the presence of Norbury; but though the body of Emmett was confined, his soul was at large; it may be that of Massillon in a royal chapel; it may be that of Cameron in a highland glen. The true speaker allows of nothing between his ideas and his utterance; acknowledges no dominion but the dominion of truth; entertains no fear, but the fear of God. Thus, too, it is, the poet sings, who sings with any grandeur; who rises to any theme of majesty or power. Thus, likewise, the philosopher speculates; free as the priest of the universe, he muses; and free as the priest of humanity, he teaches. Every great action, as well as every great word, which has been ennobled to memory, has relation to freedom, in the aspect of its nobleness. The same is true of suffering. It is as associated with freedom, freedom of soul, freedom of mind, freedom of decision, that endurance has dignity.

A man becomes heroic when he dares to suffer, when he chooses to suffer; a man becomes heroic when he prefers an appalling risk to an ignoble safety; he becomes heroic, when we see that what he endures, he endures, because he preferred the spiritual in him, to the animal; or because he ventured to assert a natural right, against an arbitrary law. No penalties, no contrivances can render such a man odious; he is superior to them all; he is hedged about with a kingliness, which no ignominy can break down. His chastisers may scourge, they may deride, they may cover him with filthy rags, they may thrust him into shameful places; our moral feelings do him justice, and he contracts no disgrace from his circumstances. Even slavery itself, has its truest pathos by its contrast with liberty. It is what the slave might be, that moves us, more than what he is; it is over manhood in its living tomb that we mourn. Suffering, I repeat, has its greatness and its dignity by association with liberty. Herein a story has its sadness; herein a tragedy has its grandeur; herein a character in history has its interest; herein the dungeon has light; herein the scaffold has glory. Break up this association; take suffering from will, and bind it to necessity; take suffering from a free soul, and unite it with a slavish spirit, and no force of imagination can ennoble it; it is sheer pain, from which we withhold our contemplation ; pain, which indeed we may pity and relieve, but which has nothing in it that exalts us, and nothing beyond passive fortitude, that we can admire.

But liberty has directly occasioned a vast amount of suffering ; liberty of country, liberty of conscience, liberty of person. It has cost much endurance ; it has been bought with a great price. Trace it along the line of centuries ; mark the prisons where captives for it pined ; mark the graves to which victims for it went down despairing ; mark the fields whereon its heroes battled ; mark the seas whereon they fought ; mark the exile to which they fled ; mark the burned spots where those who would not resist evil, gave up the ghost, in torture, to vindicate the integrity of their souls ; add these open sufferings to others that have found no record ; imagine, if you can, the whole ; then you have the price, only in part, of liberty ; for liberty has cost more than all these. Is it value for the price ? Consult, if you are able, the purchasers who paid it ; awaken from the prisons those who perished in them ; arouse from the graves the weary and broken-hearted by oppression ; call from the fields of blood, the myriads who chose death rather than bonds ; invoke from the caverns of the deep, those whom the ocean swallowed in braving the invader ; summon back from exile those who sank unseen in savage wilds. Pray for those to come once more to earth, who bore testimony to the truth in agony ; you will have a host of witnesses which no man can number, who all, aforetime, and through manifold affliction, maintained, even unto death, the cause of liberty. Inquire if they repent ; ask them, if the boon which they have given us, was worth the suffering with which they bought it ; ask, also, the speakers who proclaimed freedom, the thinkers who made laws for it, and the reformers who purified it, if the object for which they toiled, was worth the labor which they spent. That it was, all will exclaim with triumphant voice ; that it was, will come with one glad consent, with one sublime amen, from this glorious company of apostles, this goodly fellowship of prophets, this noble army of martyrs.

But liberty for all men, many would call a vision and a dream. Slavery for some, it may be said, is not only a necessity, but a blessing. The necessity is plain, for the state of slavery is, in its very nature, a state of compulsion. The blessing of that condition, however, is rather doubtful, which nothing but force can sustain, and to which nothing but weakness would submit. Some, it may be asserted, are not only not fit for liberty, but can never be.

This, surely, is not the doctrine of a believing Christian. God has given to all men, affections, conscience, reason, elements of improvement ; we cannot suppose, then, that he has excluded any from the most essential claims of their social nature. All may obtain a fitness for heaven ; it cannot be that any should be under an everlasting ban from the privileges of earth. I cannot connect such a doctrine with a Christian spirit ; I cannot connect it with a generous soul. Such a soul, from its noble impulses, must wish that all men should be partakers in every great blessing, and, wishing it, would believe they could be fit.

It is only the selfish and the vain, that would limit any thing which rejoices or which ennobles existence ; it is only those who are in themselves poor and mean of spirit, who desire monopoly of indulgence, or exclusiveness of privilege. Moses desired that all the Lord's people were prophets ; and that desire contains the essence of a great soul in every generation. The gratefully happy, would have all men happy ; the really virtuous, would have no man vicious ; the genuine philosopher would have all men enlightened ; the genuine saint would have all men holy ; the true freeman would have no man, if he could, a slave.

The claim of man to liberty, founded on his creation and his nature, may not be acknowledged, but it cannot be cancelled. Human laws may outrage, but they cannot silence it.   Human power may resist, but cannot subvert it.   It precedes the laws which wrong it.   It will outlive the power which disregards it.   On whatever ground violated, on whatever ground withheld, it is inherent and ineffaceable.   Man's title is his nature ; it is stamped upon his upward brow, it cannot be erased ; for God, who has lifted up the face of every man to heaven, has indelibly impressed it.   It glows in the moisture or the fire of his eye, and it cannot be extinguished ; for the immortal soul within, which flashes or which melts in the eye that burns, or that weeps, comes from the eternal spirit of the living God.

The right is as old as humanity, and will be co-existent with it.   Born with its birth, it will be extinguished only with its soul.   And the sentiment is as wide and as enduring as the right.   Liberty is an imperishable desire.   It is a desire that defies enactments, that scorns penalties, that baffles every scheme to kill it ; that goes on from age to age, to mock the silly restrictions by which men endeavor to stem the tide of an eternal principle.   The power of Deity within us, is its spirit ; the whole universe outside us, its boundless sacrament ; every object its type, and every voice its proclamation.   The congregation of all living things in earth, in air, in sea ; the very elements themselves, the chainless winds, the irrepressible torrent, the open sky, the sovereign ocean, the unbounded and the impartial sun. All these are its preachers; preachers of a universal providence; preachers of a universal God; preachers of a universal Father; preachers of a universal brotherhood; preachers of a universal liberty. O! we all long, I trust we do, for the day, the blessed day, when freedom shall at least be co-extensive with Christendom; when a slave, political or domestic, shall not tread on an atom, upon which the cross of Calvary has ever cast its shadow; when the baptism of the crucified shall be on every brow, the seal of a heavenly sonship; when the fire of a new pentecost shall melt asunder, by its divine heat of charity, the bonds which wrong or prejudice has fastened; when, to touch any spot over the wide sweep of God's christianized earth; any spot, which the Gospel of the Saviour has ever visited; which the name of the Saviour has ever sanctified; shall be, in itself, the spell of a complete deliverance, the magic of a perfect franchise.

TRUE MANHOOD;

ITS SIMPLICITY AND DIGNITY.

———◆———

My course, on this occasion, will lead me into no remote investigations. I will merely select a few qualities upon which, I think, a wise and true life greatly depends, and endeavor to show the connection of a simple spirit with these qualities, either as cause or as committant. If in conducting this moral analysis, for such it is, I shall speak with any positive distinctness, it will be in no spirit of self-security; but in that allegiance to truth and principle, which demands uncompromising utterance, even if that utterance condemn the speaker first. And when I refer to a simple spirit, I do not mean a weak one; I do not even mean a lowly or a gentle one; I mean a direct temper, a single mind; in a word, I refer to simplicity as opposed to complexity, for I take complexity to be associated with many of the most fatal errors, intellectual and moral, that enfeeble our existence, and pervert our characters.

In the beginning, then, I would mention the connection of a simple spirit with a sound judgment; and above all, in the judgment of one's self. An estimate of self may be bold, and yet modest; it may, on the contrary, be timid, and be yet aspiring. This modest boldness, if opportunity be given, commonly justifies itself by success; this aspiration, united with timidity, which, in a single word, we may call presumption, upon trial, mostly fails, and reaps the bitter fruits of mortification, and the heart-wearing wretchedness of obscurity and neglect. A true estimate of ourselves, intellectually and morally, is not only of importance as conducive to our own usefulness and peace, but as extensively conducive to the usefulness and peace of others. I do not say that this estimate can be formally and methodically made; it is of a general inward prudence, that I would speak. Some seem to have it as an instinct, while others seem always to miss it, either by too great rapidity, or too great slowness; yet the rapid mind can do much to train it by patient self-discipline, and the slow mind can do much to reach it by industrious self-exertion. But, whether minds be quick or dull, there is a wisdom of design, which must precede any decisive course of action, or it will give but broken resolutions and disjointed purposes; often, at the last, it will leave nothing complete, but ruin and

despair.   There is in society so much less prudence
than aspiration, so much more aspiration than power;
there is, too, so much mistake in the application of
power ; and at the root of all, so much self-ignorance
and self-delusion, that when we consider matters, our
wonder disappears at the madness and destruction that
ravage through the habitable places of the earth.

Before quitting this topic, there is yet another point
on which I will venture to remark.   The errors of an
unsound judgment are often set down as the mistakes
of genius.   The privilege of genius is so delightful, it is
no wonder that many should fancy it to be theirs ; and
it is no wonder that numbers should mistake, and, in
their mistake, be ruined.   Some, it is true, who had
the sacred fire perished ; but it was not the fire from
heaven which consumed them.   But when men who
labor for admiration fail to command it, and only draw
upon themselves misfortune, why should it be said, that
the world has no pity for their suffering ?   It was not
pity they demanded, but applause ; and had the applause been secured, the pity had not been needed.
Failure, from whatever cause, must needs bring sorrow.
There is either the want of power or the loss of power.
The power is not sufficient, or it is not appreciated ; it
is not adequate, or it is misapplied.   The candidate
for fame either over-estimates his ability, or he over-

estimates the public ; and though neglect be not always deserved, neither is the public always to blame. If the public have defective taste, that is a failing, but not a sin ; if great multitudes of the public prefer gross amusements to higher gratification, the man ambitious of doing a noble work is aware of this beforehand, and undertakes it with its risks.

Let us put the matter into an example. A man throbbing in his own heart with lofty designs, burning with an enthusiasm that ennobles and gladdens him, determines to embody these emotions in some work of beauty. He sets himself to labor on a picture ; he spends upon it years of toil ; he gives the last touches to that which has grown under his care from day to day ; which has lived into his companionship ; which has been the friend of his confidence ; the assuager of many a grief, the alleviator of many a pain ; now, complete in its perfected being, with hope, with pride, with exultation he calls in strangers to gaze upon the creature of his brain, the child of his fancy, the object of his love ; he calls them in to rejoice with him, that a new and beautiful existence is born into the world ; he calls them in, but he calls in vain ; the few that obey his invitation, look but coldly on, and then disappear, never to return. He has placed all his expectations here, and all is disappointed ; his treasure is turned to dross ; his fine gold has become dim ; his head grows wild, and his heart is broken. Another, with similar enthusiasm, composes a poem, and with similar anticipations he publishes it. It lies unbought on the bookseller's shelves, and the author, unthought of and unseen, starves in a garret, and dies there.

In the mean time, dwarfs, dancers, jugglers, gather in a splendid harvest of riches, and whether they want wealth or not, no person inquires, and how they spend it, no person cares. But dwarfs, dancers, and jugglers do perfectly what they undertake to do, and that is, to amuse the many, and the many accordingly pay them with enormous sums. Let dwarf, dancer, or juggler fail to interest their patrons, he or she then must starve, as surely as ever did painter or poet. Painter, poet, and such, throw themselves on a perilous adventure ; but even if they miss the height they aimed at, their labor is not entirely in vain. Their lives are not barren to others or to themselves ; to others they left instruction, and to themselves they gave an affluence of fine imaginings, which, doubtless, they would not have exchanged for the riches of Golconda. Genius, it is true, has often sunk from want of sympathy ; but if it has not gained much from society of hearty interest, it often has given as little as it gained. Genius has suffered from neglect, but frequently it has been genius misapplied; genius, in its best uses, has also suffered, but it has not seldom been from causes with which the public had nothing to do; which nothing in the public originated, and which nothing in the public could remedy or remove. Many have been deluded by brilliant aspirations, which they possessed no artistic talent to embody; many have been tortured by sensibilities, which had more of disease than capacity; and not a few have been led fatally astray by the exaggerations of their own vanity. When, therefore, we consider fairly what any or all of these have endured, when we deduct from it, what belonged to individual error or individual constitution, much will be taken from the general amount, which it is common to charge the coldness or the ingratitude of the world.

The mistake is, upon the whole, a moral one; and one which, with truth and simplicity of purpose, men would not so readily commit. For want of this truth and simplicity of purpose, men run into many other errors than those which lie in the pursuit of fame; errors which embarrass daily life, and which thicken shadows around characters, that otherwise would be estimable and lovable. And, from the same want, we make false estimates of others, as well as of ourselves. Objects in the physical world appear correctly in distance and dimensions, only to singleness and clearness of vision. Let singleness of vision be disturbed, and objects are not discerned in their true relations of magnitude or number. Let clearness of vision be obscured, and we apprehend not their natural colors or their proper outlines.

But there is a spiritual world around us, as real as the physical, and to see it truly is not less important. The lives of our fellow-men constitute this inward world, and to discern it truly, there must be a rectitude of inward sight. If this be dark, all is dark; we can have no certainty, either for caution or sympathy, and we shall constantly be wrong both in our avoidances and companionships. The man of a simple spirit may, indeed, be deceived; and in many ways, he may be deceived more readily than any other man, yet not in much that can be greatly to the injury of his peace, and nothing that can be to the injury of his worth. He is not indeed secure from mistaken judgment, but he is always free from wrong intention. He may not in every thing mark infallibly the ways of others, but he does righteously take heed to his own; he walks straight on the path of truth, and though persons may cross him or thwart him, they cannot shove him from it. And when we think how much there is in life of blinded conflict; how much there is of short-sighted striving; how much there is of evil temper; how much there is of evil-doing; how much there is of pain caused and pain borne, through these conflicts and strivings; we see that a man who avoids them, avoids being the agent and receiver of innumerable injuries, and in this alone, is at once the master of a noble wisdom. But while he thus preserves the tranquillity of his soul, his calmness is not apathy; it is the condition of the best, and of the highest action; it is the condition which leaves him the most control of his faculties, and in which his faculties can exert themselves to most advantage; it is the condition in which he can best choose the work that he can best do. For excitement and disturbance not only rob a man of his strength; they rob him yet more of his discernment.

The man of simple spirit discovers readily the friends with whom he can honestly unite, and as he chooses them upon solid grounds, he holds to them with a steady loyalty. They who are unsteady in their judgments are equally unsteady in their affections; for, as they do not well know why they give their regard, they know just as little why they should continue it. The superficial are always capricious; but they who are of simple spirit, are also of earnest spirit; they cannot lightly bestow their esteem; they cannot lightly withdraw it; and where they give at all, they give warmly, and they give fully. Their feelings are not weakened by diffusion; they are not sicklied by affectation; and when they have not the reality of sentiment, they will not assume its appearance. This earnestness and simplicity of feeling add vigor and decision to their judgment; and by a sort of rapid logic, akin almost to intuition, they detect the principle of a character with as much rectitude as facility. They inspire a confidence as strong as that which they bestow; and the worthy whom they seek are those whom they are fitted to attract.

Another condition essential to a high moral existence, to a true manhood, is rectitude of desire; and with this, too, simplicity of spirit is intimately connected. Desire is the parent of habit, and habit is the continuity of life. If the spirit be artificial, complicate, factitious, so will be the desires, so will be the habits, so will be the life. If, on the contrary, the spirit be simple, the desires will be natural, the habit will be pure, and the life will be genuine. Examine what it is that constitutes falsehood of life, and you will find that it is falsehood of habit; examine whence originates this falsehood of habit, and you will detect the cause in falsehood of desire; trace to its source the falsehood of desire, and you will discover it in perversions of the spirit. Here we must be content to stop.

But what, let me ask, is that which constitutes the falsehood of desire, that which lies at the very root of all that convulses and disorganizes the moral nature? It consists in placing good, not in the soul within a man, but in objects outside him; and this is not only a falsehood of confusion, but of absolute reversal; it reverses all just relations in the economy of man's being; it puts the accidents of it for the substance, and to these transient and limited accidents it gives in imagination the permanence and infinity which, in reality, belong only to the substance itself. This is not a mistake of degree, it is one of principle; it is not a mistake of detail, it is radical and fundamental; and when once the mistake is made, no strength of desire is inconsistent or irrational; for the stronger the desire, the more does the soul make its own power manifest, though the manifestation is made in a wrong direction. For, if I place the good of my being in an outward object, and not in my inward life, I am only acting in conformity with the inherent force of my immortal nature, by pursuing that object with an unquenchable intensity. If I place the good of my being in riches, what yearning for them can be absurd, what labor too constant or what quantity too great? If, again, I place my good in pleasures of the senses, in the pride of the eye, or the pride of life, what should hinder me from following after gratification with the most eager thirst ? what should stop me from grasping at the means to enjoy, and what should prevent my enjoying, when the means are mine ? Nothing. Grant the supposition, and the conclusion is just and right. There is no error in the conclusion ; but there is a most fatal, a most deadly one, in granting the supposition. But this is what no man will do in word ; scarcely even what any man ever did in thought ; and yet to how vast an extent do all men act upon it !

Looking at the error where it has more than common power, let us briefly examine some of its results. Since a man can never have wealth enough to fill a craving, which though resting on a limited object comes out from an unlimited soul, he is kept always repeating his efforts in the same direction. The object loses in freshness, but gains in command ; the craving becomes less vital and more devouring ; repetition retains no longer the consciousness of sensation ; and with the apathetic necessity of habit, it has acquired, also, the rapid facility of instinct. Now, it is of this and such habits, that the lives of millions are made up, and being so, they are made up of false relations. The souls whose perverted action these habits express, are out of harmony with the true ends of their own being, and are, therefore, out of harmony with the just conditions of other beings. They first put a false estimate on the things they seek, and when in mere literal possession they have gained them, they miss their highest uses and their truest good. With wealth they learn not the joy of bounty or the blessedness of giving; it brings no treasure to their hearts, nor always even plenty to their dwellings. Their affluence is princely, but their spirits are sordid; if they spend, it is with prodigality without grace; and if they give, it is with ostentation without munificence. When they must part at last with what they can no longer hold, they endow where they feel no benevolence, they bequeath where they inspired, and where they leave no affection; and whether they serve the public or enrich individuals, the public hold their examples in no reverence, and individuals attach no sacredness to their memories. And this false medium is but one out of many, in which men vainly follow after good; and while busy in this " strenuous idleness," they think not that real good can only dwell within the living soul; that it can dwell there only as that living soul aspires toward its highest destiny; that these aspirations can only have sufficiency in the Perfect — in God, and in all things as they reveal him; in his creation, in his providence; in pure minds, in great minds; in every being through which he reflects the divinity of wisdom, and the glow of beauty.

Men of just and simple spirits do not undervalue any thing in life. They shrink not from the wealth, the occupations, the struggles, the distinctions, the enjoyments of the world ; and they are willing to risk all the obligations, the vicissitudes, the mistakes, and the sufferings which attach to the pursuit of them. But they never confound the accessories of fortune with the essence of happiness, or take the scale of station for the scale of dignity. They understand well how from such things to extract the noblest uses ; but they never think of them as sources of lofty or lasting happiness. The highest gratifications are not those which money can procure, nor those which the want of it can hinder ; the highest gratifications are those of which the means are given freely, and the means, so far as the dispensations of nature are concerned, are distributed with a most bountiful equality. We need but health and a moderate subsistence ; then, with simple tastes, the world is to us a resplendent dwelling, a richly furnished home ; we have then a vast property in the works of God, we are lords of a magnificent possession ; and to the utmost capacity of our faculties, the past, the present, the mighty universe, are our inheritance. The stars give all their joy without a price to those who look up to them in a wakeful spirit, and when their beams meet in the clear eye a radiance from the soul within, to that soul the whole arch of heaven becomes a blaze of living glory. Can gold or gems present so rich a splendor? Can art prepare so fair a show as these solemn heavens, which God, himself, stretcheth out as a curtain, which he spreadeth abroad as a tent to dwell in?

These solemn heavens are for the poorest, who will turn to them in faith and contentment from the lowliest cottage-porch. They are the same heavens which patriarchs loved to watch when men yet walked with their Creator; they are the same heavens, upon which the prophets gazed with souls inspired, when they waited for the Creator's visions; they are the same heavens which David in his raptures sung. Not to speak more fully of outward nature, there are other riches, too, in which we need none of us be deficient; the treasures of the affections, the bounties of friendship, the replenishment of all cordial emotions, the wealth of all generous sentiments.

The circle which I have here described, is not a small one; a life needs not go beyond it, and be a very noble life, and yet it will be a very simple life. It calls for no excessive culture; it requires no peculiar sensibilities; it implies no extraordinary circumstances; it does not necessarily belong to this station or to that; a prince may live it, or a peasant, and we hope that many a prince and many a peasant does live it. There are other means of pure enjoyment, that seem only to be within the compass of the wealthy — books, pictures, statues, diversities of travel, and varieties of intercourse with mankind. These are not essentials to a mind that has a vital being within itself, and that has a vital relation to being outside it. They are often but the toys that amuse indolence, and not the objects of manly study; often but luxuries to the jaded senses, and not the food of a healthy appetite. A living mind has that within it and around, out of which books are made, from which paintings are drawn, and from which sculptures are shaped; thoughts and fancies, numberless; landscapes of infinite outline, colorings, and forms, with all the lights and shadows of the changing year; men and women, with all the strength, and grace, and loveliness, which art delights to copy.

It must be a barren region that will not be rich to natural sensibility, though it should never traverse others; and that must be a dull community which, to a reflective spirit, will not be an epitome of his kind. But these things, whatever be their worth, are fast coming within the grasp of all. A simple cast reveals to us, however faintly, the serene sublimity which Phidias chiseled; a print, not expensive, brings to our eyes, though with imperfect vision, the sacred beauty of which Raffael dreamed ; steam gives us journeyings, and steam gives us books. He must be, indeed, an indigent man, who cannot place more wisdom and more poetry upon his shelf, than all his years can fathom or exhaust ; and this he can easily do, though he should place there no other volumes, than Defoe, Bunyan, Shakspeare, and the Bible. After the certainty of shelter and subsistence, every man can be truly rich in whatever constitutes the goodliest treasure of humanity. There is no real destitution, but poverty of spirit, and poverty of heart.

We think upon our subject in one aspect more, the connection of a simple spirit with rectitude of principle. A just man is always simple. He is a man of direct aims and purposes. There is no complexity in his motives, and, thence, there is no jarring or discordancy in his character. He wishes to do right, and in most cases he does it ; he may err, but it is by mistake of judgment, and not by perversity of intention. The moment his judgment is enlightened, his action is corrected. Setting before himself, always, a clear and worthy end, he will never pursue it by any concealed or unworthy means. We may carry our remarks for illustration, both into private and into public life. Observe such a man in his home ; there is a charm about him, which no artificial grace has ever had the power to bestow ; there is a sweetness, I had almost said, a music in his manners, which no sentimental refinement has ever given. His speech, ever fresh from purity and rectitude of thought, controls all that are within its hearing, with an unfelt, and yet a resistless sway. Faithful to every domestic trust, as to his religion and his God, he would no more prove recreant to any loyalty of home, than he would blaspheme the Maker in whom he believes, or than he would forswear the heaven in which he hopes. Fidelity and truth to those bound by love and nature to his heart, are to him most sacred principles ; they throb in the last recesses of his moral being, they are imbedded in the life of his life ; and to violate them, or even think of violating them, would seem to him as a spiritual extermination, the suicide of his soul. Nor is such a man unrewarded, for the goodness that he so largely gives, is largely paid back to him again ; and though the current of his life is transparent, it is not shallow ; on the contrary, it is deep and strong. The river that fills its channel, glides smoothly along in the power of its course ; it is the stream which scarcely covers the ruggedness of its bed, that is turbulent and noisy. With all this gentleness, there is exceeding force ; with all this meekness, there is imperative command ; but the force is the force of wisdom, and the command is the command of

gives a moment to silent prayer; he meekly lays his head upon the block; then, there is the echo of a blow that sends a soul to heaven!

I have traced rectitude of spirit, and rectitude of life, through the several gradations of a sublime example, and found it, at every stage, connected with simplicity. The example is not imaginary; it is real, it is practicable. I have had, all the time, an original before my mind's eye; but I have faintly conceived the original, and I have yet more faintly embodied my conception. The original is, Sir Thomas More, one of England's greatest, as well purest, chancellors; and to bring out distinctly all the beauty of his character, would require much more than a lecture, and powers far transcending mine. "Of all men nearly perfect," says Sir James Mackintosh, "Sir Thomas More had, perhaps, the clearest marks of individual character. His peculiarities, though distinguishing him from all others, were yet withheld from growing into moral faults. It is not enough to say of him, that he was unaffected, that he was natural, that he was simple; so the larger part of truly great men have been. But there is something homespun in More, which is common to him with scarcely any other, and which gives to all his faculties and qualities the appearance of being the natural growth of the soil. The homeliness of his pleasantry purifies it from show.

He walks on the scaffold clad in his household goodness. The unrefined benignity with which he ruled his dwelling at Chelsea, enabled him to look on the axe without being disturbed by hatred for the tyrant. This quality bound together his genius and learning, his eloquence and fame with his homely and daily duties, bestowing a genuineness on all his good qualities, a dignity on all the offices of life, and an accessible familiarity on the virtues of a martyr and a hero, which silences every suspicion that his excellencies were magnified. He, thus, simply performed great acts, and uttered great thoughts, because they were familiar to his great soul. The charm of this inborn and home-bred character, seems as if it would be taken off by polish. It is this household character which relieves our notion of him from vagueness, and divests perfection of that generality and coldness, to which the attempt to paint a perfect man is so liable."

If the aim of a life be right, it cannot in detail be much amiss. It may indeed be imperfect, but it cannot be wholly wrong, and it cannot even partially be false. When the aim of a life is right, rules and precepts are merely subordinate ; when the aim of a life is otherwise, rules and precepts are utterly worthless. Lord Bacon, the great master of modern wisdom, with that incomparable union of practical philosophy and luxuriant poetry, which distinguished him amongst all the teachers of mankind, instructs us on this point thus: for he says, — " If these two things be supposed, that a man set before him honest and good ends; and again, that he be resolute and constant, and true unto them, it will follow that he will mould himself into all virtue at once ; and this indeed is the work of nature. * * * * For as when a carver makes an image, he shapes only that part whereupon he worketh ; (as if he be upon the face, that part which shall be the body is but rude stone still, till such time as he come to it ;) but contrariwise when nature makes a flower or a living creature, she formeth rudiments of all the parts at once. So in obtaining virtue by habit, while a man practiseth temperance he doth not profit much to fortitude ; but when he dedicateth and applieth himself to good ends, to what virtue soever the pursuit and passage toward those ends doth command him, he is invested with a precedent disposition to conform himself thereunto."

The author of this fine passage presents in his own practice, by contrast and negation, an illustration of its truth. For if a man have not right and good ends, any excellence in his nature is but poor and partial ; if he give himself to one evil end, basely and progressively, deeply and more deeply, all the cognate vices follow.

Bacon, in his conduct, toiled for unworthy ends, and he, accordingly, shrunk not from the use of degrading and dishonest means. His character stands in broad contrast, indeed, to that of Sir Thomas More ; and the moral contrast is rendered all the more glaring, from some points between them of social similarity.

I do not mention intellectual analogy, because there was none. Both, to be sure, were men of genius ; but the genius of Bacon, intellectually regarded, was to the genius of More, as the expanse of meridian day is to the radiance of the morning star. But the moral elevation of More above Bacon is as transcendent as the intellectual majesty of Bacon above the commonest of men. Bacon was not loved in his home ; and in friendship he was equally disloyal and ungrateful. The generous patron, who aided him on his way to power, he not only forsook, but resisted, and that in the hour of his calamity. He did not, as More, manfully stand up for public rights in the face of danger ; nor brave, as More did, the anger of two hereditary tyrants. Bacon, without any risk, gratuitously cringed to the sycophants of Elizabeth and the parasites of James. It was not even to the personalities of the despots themselves that he made a willing sacrifice of his manhood, but to their most contemptible subordinates ; with an intellect fitted for the priesthood of all nature, he paid submissive homage to the shadows of a queenly termagant, and to the favorites of a royal fool. Bacon sought office with as much desire as More avoided it ; Bacon used as much solicitation to obtain it, as More endured to accept it, and each, when in it, was equally true to his character. More was as simple, as Bacon was ostentatious. More was as incorruptible, as Bacon was venal. More spent his private fortune in office, and Bacon spent the wages of corruption there. Both left office poor in worldly good ; but while More was rich in honor and good deeds, Bacon was poor in every thing ; poor in the mammon for which he bartered his integrity ; poor in the gawd for which he sacrificed his peace ; poor in the presence of the worthless ; covered with shame in the midst of the people ; trusting his fame to posterity, of which posterity is only able to say, that the wisest of men was adviser to the silliest of kings, yet that such a king had a sort of majesty when morally compared with the official director of his conscience. Both More and Bacon served each a great purpose for the world. More illustrated the beauty of holiness ; Bacon expounded the infinitude of science. Bacon became the prophet of intellect ; More, the martyr of conscience. The one pours over our understandings the light of knowledge ; but the other inflames our hearts with the love of virtue.

Contrasts besides these will suggest themselves to the minds of my hearers. There is one, especially, which they will not fail to recall ; and that is, the complicated policy and theatrical splendor of Napoleon, in connection with the simple patriotism and the massive wisdom of Washington. The dazzling and impassioned career of the one, at the end as barren as the rock on which he died ; the steady and disinterested course of the other, finished amidst the tears and blessings of the millions to whom he gave a nation. The one standing out to futurity only in the singleness of his own personality, clad, in the might of his terrible genius, with slaughter, and flames, and ruin proclaiming his conquests, while the wail of nations called for his exile, and the fear of mankind kept him in it ; the other, retiring from individual greatness, and hiding, if possible, the glory of renown in the benignity of his triumphs ; arising upon our grateful memories, not in the costume of sanguinary warfare, but of philanthropic peace ; not in the pomp of an imperial dictator, but in the modesty of a simple citizen ; not in the fiery brilliancy of death-spreading victories, but in the calmer light of life-giving institutions — the father of his country, the benefactor of the world.

I have dwelt on this longer than I intended. It had been sufficient to merely hint it ; for the contrast is so obvious, and has been so often drawn, that more than an allusion is scarcely graceful, and yet some allusion could hardly be avoided ; but all serve to illustrate my general position, that simplicity is ever an element in the highest manhood. Without this, greatness may indeed be stupendous, but it is not harmonious ; its presence may be resistless, but it does not attract to itself willing, cordial, welcome memories. It signifies not, how vast the intellect, how enriched the imagination, how extraordinary the power, how immense the achievement ; they fail in that unity and pleasure of impression, which the greatness always leaves that men delight to honor ; the greatness that, by affection, gives life to admiration, and that secures an immortal remembrance by an immortal love.

The idea with which I would close, is inferred in nearly all that I have said ; the connection of a simple spirit with solid independence and genuine dignity. For, if it be connected with soundness of judgment, with rectitude of desire, and rectitude of principle, then it is connected with all that constitutes the very essence of independence and of dignity. The man of a simple spirit is saved from the mistakes of vanity, from mistakes of doubtful purpose ; and these are the mistakes that most embarrass a life, mistakes, the readiest to deceive, and the hardest to be cured. The man of a simple spirit is not misled by factitious or superfluous desires, which wreck so much of peace, and which spread so much of misery. How silently and fearfully can such influences gather round a man, until, before he knows that he is in captivity, he is corded and chained in the most humiliating, the most debasing slavery! They entangle his circumstances; they undermine his integrity; they enfeeble his moral sense; they blunt his feelings of honor; they bow down the erectness of his self-respect; until his life is a hard struggle for outward seeming, or the last contempt even of appearances; a constant remorse without the power to amend, or the final despair that has given up the hope or the inclination to change.

The moral nature is that, which, in the highest sense, constitutes the man. Faithful to this, the man is true; unfaithful to it, he is false. Now this, I say, belongs, not to the class, not to the profession, not to the office, but distinctly to the man.

The moral feelings, then, are those in which a man is greatest; not alone, because they are those in which he is most spiritual, but because they are those in which he is most independent. These are his without hindrance or limitation; they are his, absolutely and supremely. The moral feelings need no external instrumentality; they are complete in themselves. The command of conscience to the will, and the answer of the will in obedience to it, constitute the perfection and sufficiency of virtue. This nothing can limit or destroy. A right will is right action; and though such a will be the movement of a spirit imprisoned in a body all paralyzed and moveless, it is stronger than the universe.

Is not this a grand privilege of man, immortal man, that though he may not be able to stir a finger; that though a moth may crush him; that merely by a righteous will, he is raised above the stars; that by it he originates a good in the universe, which the universe could not annihilate; a good which can defy extinction, though all created energies of intelligence or matter, were combined against it? It is not thus with the desires and appetites; they do need an outward instrumentality. Without the outward instrumentality, they become occasions of uneasiness and pain, and with it in the utmost fullness, they yet have no perfection. But a man whose moral nature is ascendant, commands these. He is not the subject, but the superior of circumstances. He is free; nay more, he is a king; and though this sovereignty may have been won by many desperate battles, once on the throne, and holding the sceptre with a firm grasp, he has a royalty of which neither time nor accident can strip him.

Years do not enfeeble, they ennoble it; they do not
dim, they brighten it; they surround it with the halo of
a purer atmosphere, and they draw men to do more
affectionate homage to its venerable beauty. Mutability
comes not near it; there is no power that it has cause
to fear; there is no enemy that can prevail against it.
It is the only royalty which revolutions cannot over-
turn.

Neither does earthly estate interfere with its dominion
or its grandeur.   In the dungeon or on the rack, at
the stake or on the scaffold, it contracts no infamy from
its situation; nay, it is the more resplendent in its kingliness.   It is not often found in palaces, but when within
them, it is their finest presence.   It does not always
rule in the breasts of monarchs; but when it does, it
marks them truly for the Lord's anointed.   It is the
real inspiration of a princely nature; and where it is
absent, a star is but a dazzling blotch, and a sceptre
but a mischievous or a foolish bauble.   It has no sure
promise of worldly goods; it is not always attended
with outward prosperity; it has not always gay dwellings, and sometimes it has none; it needs no show of
outward pomp; it has no regal costume, no regal ban-
quets; it does not, by any virtue of its dignity, wear
purple and fine linen, or fare sumptuously every day;
but without whereon to lay its head, it may yet be

our own country or Europe, who have paid attention to the physical or spiritual condition of the poor. What hordes of human beings in London, on whom the Sabbath sun never dawns with the gladness of religion, on whose ears the church-going bell never sounds with the music of peace ! We know it to be ˈasserted as a certainty, and we have no reason to think it otherwise, that thousands in London have never crossed the threshold of a church or chapel. Suppose, then, two persons to take different directions in a great city during the hours of divine service ; one to the churches, the other to the dwellings of the poor, and the retreats of vice ; on comparison of notes, which would be found the most crowded ? We fear the result. Yet all not at worship would not be found in guilt. Many are dead in the insensibility of ignorance, born to darkness, they have fulfilled their destiny ; many without provision for the wants of nature, forget those wants which are latest and deepest ; many from shame-faced delicacy will not go in raggedness to the congregation of their neighbors, nor let those who once knew them otherwise see them in their fall and wretchedness.

Turning then from those who are absent by extreme ignorance or extreme indigence, let us refer for a moment to those, who are neither ignorant nor indigent ; who remain away from the mere want of inclination or

inducement to attend.   To the former class we shall
allude again, before we close this article ; of the latter,
we may consider that no small portion of it is to be
found in the intelligent and independent working population.   Thousands we believe of this class, both in our
own country and Europe, rarely go to church.   And
how, it may be inquired, are they in the mean time
engaged ? Variously.   Some walk into the fields ; some
instruct their families ; some give themselves to private
study ; and others attend philosophical debates.   The
rapid and extensive progress of Owenism among the
operatives of Britain is an evidence to which nothing
stronger can be added.   Shall we find the case otherwise among the higher classes ?   In America and England, where attendance on public worship is a matter of
decorum, where such attendance is commonly a sine-
qua-non of respectable station, few that desire to stand
fairly with society will entirely desert the house of
prayer.

But look to France, and other countries on the
European continent, and where conventional scru-
ple does not operate in the same manner, and you
see churches all but empty.   Exceptions there are,
such as those we alluded to before, but literally they
are exceptions.   M. Coquerel, with his fine delivery
and polished eloquence, is surrounded with the Protes-

tant élite of Paris ; and a few years ago, when M. Cordaire, patronized by the young men, was the fashion, his church was thronged with the aristocracy of Catholicism. So was it with Edward Irving in London ; a mob of nobility, senators, and statesmen pressed about him to suffocation, but the time soon came, when the magic could charm no more ; and when, after a life exhausted before its prime, he sought his mother-land to die, he had been long forgotten by the courtly circles. While his eloquent eccentricities had novelty they went to hear him, as they would a new prima donna at the opera ; curiosity gratified and taste satiated, they had nothing else to desire ; deserted on all sides, he laid his head among those who knew in private his manly and Christian worth; who were not held merely by the lambency of his genius, and did not with the crowd depart, when the lights began to fail. Numbers of professional men are habitually indifferent to the pulpit, with whom, however unjust it may be considered, a sermon is but another name for an opiate. Rare talents may draw them forth, but rare talents, as implied in the very epithet, are scattered over wide intervals both of time and space. Looking, therefore, from one extreme of society to the other, and taking any part of Christendom as our field of observation, we think the fact established, that the pulpit, — not of this sect or that,

— but the general modern pulpit, to a large extent, has lost, or is losing, its power. If such be the fact, what the cause or causes ? We shall, to the best of our power, endeavor to explain.

The first reason we shall assign is extrinsic to the pulpit, and is founded in the growing influence which progressive civilization has been giving to the press. Previous to the reformation and the invention of printing, the priesthood was the depository of all knowledge that existed, and the only medium for its utterance. The pulpit was then the single and solitary source of popular instruction, and around it was the submissive throng of believing multitudes ; uninquiring faith listened to its mandates, and princes, equally with the people, bent before its authority. The instrument of moral teaching, the peculiar dispenser of religious thought, it was, moreover, the only means of civilization. When we consider the gross ignorance of the lower classes, as then existing ; the equal ignorance of the lay nobility, with ferocious and despotic passions superadded ; if it were not for the impressive sanctions of religion, and the influence of preaching, we know not how society could have been preserved from the most frightful and savage anarchy. Whatever raised men above their grossest and their worst propensities ; whatever restrained them in their fiercest and most unlawful desires ;

whatever softened or humanized their manners; whatever nurtured or diffused the best charities of life, were mainly or entirely in those ages gathered from the pulpit. The pulpit was the people's protector, as well as instructor; the only power which could make the despot quail; a power, before which the mightiest monarch became weak in presence of the most lowly monk. The priest may have often been a tyrant, but most commonly he was the tyrant of the tyrant; and the hand of the oppressor, filled with blood and plunder, has not seldom been broken by the lightning of the church. In such times, it was well to have a power which feared neither knights nor kings; a power which, in its very supremacy over worldly rank, could humiliate the great and protect the poor. When we fling sarcasms at the priesthood unsparing and unjust, we do not probably recollect, how much popular rights awe such men as Becket and Langton. While slavery and silence, except when speech was to flatter or to lie, prevailed in courts and senates, the pulpit was the only place where free and fearless utterance found a refuge; where men, who almost claimed the reverence of gods, were taught to feel they were but brothers of the worm, made of the same earth with the meanest serf that crouched before them in the dust. Preachers may have abused their office and been false to their mission, may

have been bigots, fanatics, persecutors ; but their worst
enemy, if he has any candor, cannot say that as a body
they have feared to proclaim what they believed the
truth.   That many of them at all times have been
hypocrites, sycophants, there is no denying ; but if
hypocrisy and sycophancy are to be taken as points of
comparison, the history of the church, bad as it is, need
but little fear the contrast with that of any other prominent social institution.

The art of printing introduced a new element into
society ; but, for a long period, this was remote as the
stars from the people.   The reformation itself, though
greatly aided among the learned by the press, was principally diffused among the people by the pulpit ; books
were the sources in which the learned found knowledge ;
but preaching was the stream on which it flowed down
to the vulgar ; in books the seeds of new thoughts were
garnered, but oral discourse was the wind which carried
them far and wide to germinate over an expansive soil.

There were two parts in this mighty work, as there
must always be in every great moral revolution in
which documentary evidence is concerned ; the analytic
and descriptive ; the critical and the expositional ; the
one the department of learning, the other of eloquence.
Luther, in his own person, gives us an instance of the
two offices combined ; Luther, in his closet or his

castle, the translator of the Bible ; Luther, in his pulpit or his chair, the impetuous and irresistible expounder. Preaching was therefore the main instrument by which the Protestant Reformation was sent forth among the people ; its sermons, lectures, and disputes, from Geneva to Glasgow, and from Wirtemberg to Paul's cross, aroused the popular mind to action and revolt ; it gave the sound which called the people to the battle, and that which once had proclaimed the glory of Rome, gathered the storm which shattered its throne. Religious freedom, as well as general civilization, has derived impulse from the pulpit, and the movement, which has carried millions into moral independence, was born in the thunder which a Luther or a Knox rolled forth upon the world. As civil liberty is generally either the consequence or the companion of religious independence, so far as the pulpit has advanced the latter, it has likewise advanced the former. Up to this point, then, we see in the pulpit the principal source of instruction, of social civilization, of moral revolution ; but from this point we observe another order of things gradually taking place.

The press, as we before noticed, was at first only the privilege of the educated, and the educated were the wealthy. So it continued to be until a very recent period. Mr. Foster, in his " Essay on Popular

Ignorance," observes that even in the time of Addison there could scarcely be said to be " a reading public." We quote from memory, but we give the substance of his remark.   We think its truth will not be disputed by those who compare that period with ours ; for surely the wits for whom wits wrote, the fine gentlemen and fine ladies, the fops and dilettanti, who waited for their daily portion of pungent gossip or graceful satire, in the Tattler or Spectator, are not to be called " a public," if we are to give the same designation to the earnest millions who, at the present day, devour such periodicals as Chambers's Journal.   Even politics — always topics of popular interest — had not numerous readers and students in the laboring classes.   Swift, Junius, and Wilkes, writers who in their time created more excitement than perhaps any other three that could be named in the history of party, were not read, it is probable, by the twentieth part of those with whom they were idols. Multitudes of the people are now readers, not of morbid or maudlin trash, but of many of the best productions of our religious, philosophical, and general literature. Time was, when it was considered an act of mighty wisdom and philanthropy, to place within the poor man's reach some history of " Jack and Tom," of " The Two Apprentices," " The Infidel Cobler," with others of similar taste and elevation ; and if the humble reader, or rather speller, had not the grace to be pleased with these, he was met on the other side only by the spawnings of obscenity and indecency. That time, we trust, is gone. We remember ourselves, when the tracts of Hannah More were considered by the patrons of the poor, as the very perfection of cottage reading. We mention this in no spirit of disrespect, for we think that the effort to interest her fellow-creatures in virtue deserves well of posterity ; we adduce it merely to show that taste has been progressively rising. That it was not higher was no fault of hers, while hers was all the praise to lower her powers to its level.

The tendency, therefore, of circumstances has been to give increasing influence to the press. Rich in present and past intellect, its facilities of diffusion are abundant beyond measure. Its cheap and rapid machinery transcends all that superstition had ever conceived of magic. The amount of production is in proportion to the facilities of diffusion, and both go forward with an accelerating ratio. Every variety of work is to be found in every variety of edition ; periodicals for every purpose and for every class ; and resorts for reading, where, in other times, nothing had been but gross ribaldry and savage ignorance. Books are now to be seen from the cellar to the garret, and knowledge has made its way, where the sun himself had scarcely pierced. Unseen and unsuspected, an under current of inquiry has been flowing with steady course and increasing strength, and the seeds of thought have fructified before it was suspected they had been sown. Knowledge, that was only the rich man's companion, has become the poor man's friend; seeks him in the factory and workshop, enlightens his home and dignifies his occupations. She accompanies the peasant to his lonely haunts, fills his solitude with thought, trains his ear to the music of heaven, and his eye to the goodliness of nature. The voice of knowledge is gone forth over the earth in every civilized language; her cry is heard from the Alps to the Andes, and in every space between. The pulpit, accordingly, is no longer the exclusive instrument of popular instruction; books divide the power, and to a certain extent all but monopolize it.

The progress of the press, as we have shown, divides power with the pulpit as a moral teacher. We shall state two causes incidental to the pulpit's own administration, which, more than any external circumstances, limit its influence and usefulness, namely, sameness and sectarianism.

First, we say sameness, and we shall endeavor to explain and justify our meaning. Preaching, as we find it in popular pulpits, is monotonous almost beyond endurance. And that such intellectual uniformity should coexist with much religious division, seems a kind of moral paradox; but so it is. If we take that form of religion, the most popular in these times, termed evangelical, it will be sufficient for our purpose. An evangelical discourse is not a sermon, but a system; and this system, running along the whole line of theology, from the fall of man in Eden to his beatification in heaven, or his perdition in hell, is jumbled into half an hour's or an hour's declamation, repeated from Sunday to Sunday, and church to church, without novelty of argument or freshness of illustration, until the mind droops in very weariness, and the ear grows tired of the sound. From this, in most popular churches, there is no retreat. The form of worship may be different; ecclesiastical form or discipline may vary; the talents of the preachers may vary, but the evangelical sermon is identical in all; commonly a variegated series of texts, held together by a thread of very common-place, or very fanciful analogy. And many, we apprehend, would think the minister unfaithful to his trust, and that the Gospel was not savingly preached, was there omitted an important article of their peculiar faith. Thus the sphere of pulpit thought and action is circumscribed within the narrowest limits; Christian speech is shackled by the bonds of system; and the wonderful wealth of the Bible is reduced to a few disjointed texts. The pulpit thunders with boisterous tameness, but in its noise the inward sighings of the natural conscience are unheard, the deeper sorrows of the heart unsolaced, and the trials of life overlooked, or but vaguely noticed.

When we complain of sameness in the ministrations of the general pulpit, let it not be thought that we make an unjust demand for variety. To expect from the pulpit the same exciting novelty in preaching, as in other species of literature, would be uncandid and unfair. The temptations arising from gain and ambition, are more in the direction of any other profession than the clerical, and therefore, to such professions, a great portion of the most distinguished talent will, of course, be attracted. The clerical profession, also, requires a numerous body of men to supply the moral wants of the Christian community; naturally the majority must be but of average ability, and by the very necessity of circumstances consist of men respectable, rather than eminent in intellect. Besides, they labor under many trials and disadvantages. The necessity of periodical composition is, in itself alone, no slight aggravation of ministerial toil. Who, that has ever experienced the necessity of stated intellectual preparation, will not understand this? The head may be heavy with bodily disease, or the heart sick with inward grief; the pen may tremble in the hand, and the eye grow dim with sorrow; but the shadow of the Sabbath is already upon their imagination, and the weekly sermon must be ready. Alas! the tale of brick must be forthcoming, and often there is not wherewith to make it; yet hundreds of upturned faces will be upon the pastor in the temple, to seek for direction and support in their pilgrimage, when he, who is expected to dispense, may be the being of all present who most needs them. How often will the sense of this responsibility scare ministers in their dreams and break their sleep, oppress them in society, and follow them into solitude.

The very difficulty of composition is itself a labor, which those who have not tried can but feebly estimate; and men of worldly business are not always aware at what expense of anxious and painful meditation the discourse was completed, which, in hearing, seemed so simple and so fluent. Persons accustomed to one sort of labor, are bad judges of those whose sphere of action is specifically different from their own; the man of bodily energy is therefore little conscious of the toil of him, who spends his strength and wears out his life in the solitude of the study. Bustling about in the thoroughfare of the world, jostling and jostled, the study seems to him no more than a quiet and indolent retreat; but he forgets that in that retreat there is an ever-flowing current of thought wearing away its embankments ; and that the soul, stimulated in all its faculties, may be beating its tenements to atoms.

Ministers have to choose their own subjects; and although rhetoricians reckon this as one of their privileges, those who know human nature well will class it among their disadvantages.   They must therefore, to interest strongly, have that sort of originality which can unceasingly draw forth fresh subjects of thought, or by illustration throw new interest around the old ; the latter probably the more difficult.   Now in the other oratorical professions, the speaker has the subject ready at his hand ; and commonly it is one with which his hearers immediately sympathize.   The lawyer has his case prepared by the events that require his interference ; and if he be at all a man of talent, from their very circumstantiality, he can readily invest them with a dramatic interest.   The senator's oration is suggested by the bill which his party or the times devise.   The actor has the character he is to personate sculptured for him by the imagination of his author ; but the preacher must weekly propose his own case ; and to make deep impression on cultivated minds, he must argue it with the logic of the lawyer or the legislator, and deliver it with the grace and propriety of the actor. Then comes the difference of remuneration.   This is indeed the least consideration to an honorable man in any liberal profession; although it is something to have a life of arduous exertion crowned with an age of independent competency, instead of relying on willing or unwilling subscription, which is the end of many a clergyman's career. But there is another kind of reward dear to every man of honest zeal, and that is to be certain that his labor has not been in vain. On this point the preacher may be unassured to the very close of life. The lawyer is satisfied when his cause is gained, the senator when his bill is passed, the actor when his audience laughs or weeps; they have definite purposes, and they have definite tests, by which to know when these purposes are effected. With a minister it is not so; he must often cast his bread upon the waters, and not find it until after many days indeed; nay, with best intentions, he may sink at last under the weight of apparent failure.

We can easily conceive a young man cast alone into some distant and retired spot. He enters on his work with ardor, with talent, and with hope. He speaks from a true and loving heart, and endeavors, with all sincerity, to realize his beautiful ideal of ministerial devotedness. With a growing family his wants increase, and poverty at last besets him. Necessity drives him to the weekly drudgeries of a

school ; cares and crosses gather round a perplex-
ed intellect; his periods of composition are the hours
stolen from his rest, the intervals of his slavery ; his
youth departs ; his heart dies within him ; novelty of
thought expires in the dull monotony of his life ; his
energy tames down to mediocrity ; his eloquence di-
lutes to commonplace ; his hearers gradually retire,
except, perhaps, a few who remain from pity or from
habit ; with little sympathy at hand, and no fame at a
distance, with a worn spirit and shattered expectations,
he finds his position a solitude — a solitude, not of
apathy but of agony. The feelings of the gentleman
and the scholar are not dead ; the spectres of his once
bright fancyings crowd about his tortured imagination ;
his former generous ambition turns into moody disappointment ; at last he occupies an unminded grave in
his own secluded church-yard, or he lives until another
generation knows him not ; knows nothing of the once
glowing preacher in the old and jaded schoolmaster.

And such is the true history of many a minister's
course. We make the admission, that failure may
attend, or seem to attend, the best exertions ; but we
think that, in general, the cause will be found in some
faults of talent or of temper. The preacher must
bring to his work the spirit of love as well as the spirit
of power. Associated with his hearers in the most

impressive eras of life, in Sabbath worship, in birth, in death, and in the consecration of wedded love, if he be faithful to his trust, and unite the warmth of a friend to the zeal of a minister, the circumstances must indeed be peculiar, in which pastoral industry can lose its just reward; but should there be no return from the world, there is that within the soul itself in the consciousness of fulfilled duty, which, as the world does not give, neither can it take away.

Setting aside, therefore, all undue craving for variety, the human mind fairly demands a certain portion of it, and for all that is necessary to sustain a religious and moral interest, the pulpit affords abundant opportunities and resources. The objects which are its topics are the greatest in existence, before which the outward world is lost in immensity; God, eternity, the human soul; all that concerns duty here, and all that concerns destiny hereafter. The preacher, like the prophet in the mount, must behold the creatures and scenes around him with unsealed vision; and when the eye of flesh can only see the things of earth and time, his must pierce the veil of matter and mortality. To him, the world is full of undying souls, with endless consciousness and endless capacity; to him, all being has its highest worth, as it stands related to the greatest goodness and the greatest happiness; to him, the sublimest

view of this mighty globe itself is, that it is the place
where a deathless humanity is cradled for the skies,
the place where God unfolds his dispensations, and
where he is conducting an all-wise providence to everlasting purposes. Its topics are therefore exhaustless;
everlasting in their importance as they are everlasting
in their nature. For, what is the mission of the pulpit
but the mission of Christ continued ? — a mission to the
human conscience, and the human soul, to win, to warn,
to instruct, to inspire men with love for the true, the
right, the pure, the beautiful, and the good ; to draw
them from the corrupt influences of selfishness and
passion ; to denounce iniquity in spirit and in action;
with the mercy of Jesus, to seek the outcast, to save
the lost, to labor for the worst ; in the hour of private
calamity or public suffering to be a messenger of peace
to the hearts of the afflicted ; to direct the downcast eye
to the bow of hope, spanning the dreary horizon with
the gleam of promise ; to awaken in deepest sorrow
the spirit of faith, and banish the demon of despair,
even when earth is as iron, and heaven as brass.

The circumstances, too, which accompany the ministration of the pulpit, are as impressive as its purpose is
sublime. The day is sacred and tranquil, when cheerfulness and rest soften the harshness of toil, and thoughts
of a better destiny will flash across the most worldly

soul. Prayer is present with all its humanizing tenderness, and music also, with its holiest inspiration. The audience around the pulpit, next `to that which shall stand before the judgment-seat of Christ, are in the most solemn of all relations. Gathered from all ranks` and conditions, they are there equal as in the slumber of the grave ; their earthly destinations and differences, the toys and titles, for which they value themselves or are valued by others, are, or aught to be, nothing there ; there they are assembled, not as distinguished or ob scure, but as children of God ; as strangers and sojourners on earth, looking for their home and rest in heaven. All the associations of the place are connected with duty and immortality; and the truths to which it is dedicated, however rudely or feebly uttered, are solemn beyond measure. And man, within sight of the pulpit, is always in a position to be revered, never to be scorned ; not as he sometimes is even in legislative assemblies, where selfish and mean interests will often assume the sacred name of wisdom ; where intellectual splendor but too frequently throws a fiercer glow around moral deformity, and where the conflict of faction kindles all that is worst in the worst passions ; not as in a court of justice, where every view of man has something fearful in it, whether we regard it in the culprit covered with guilt, or the judge clothed in terror.

The orator of the pulpit has a wide and varied sphere, if he but use the materials it affords. He has the conscience and the heart; he can enter their secret retirements. With a deep study of his own nature; with an eye that has not perused in vain the history of human life, nor gazed vacantly on its myriad forms of character, he can pierce the bosom, depict its struggles, describe its dangers, trace the sources of sin and suffering. And in this little world alone, what infinite diversity, not only in the forms of virtue, but of temptation, guilt, remorse, misery; all that makes the moral history of sin, all that makes the tragedy of life. The preacher has human homes to which, as we have said before, he is bound by most sacred bonds. When affliction has softened the spirit; when experience has made the most common truths impressive, and translated with deep meaning to the heart, what before had been lifeless to the ear; when the lights are quenched in the hall, and tears are in the place of feasting, and the death-bed with all its solemn scenery, is amidst the surviving and the loved; yet, not these only, but also whatever brightens or blesses the dwelling; smiling infancy; sportive childhood; the joy and duty of parents; the blessed charities of this life, and holy hopes of the next; all these are his, and which simply to feel is to be eloquent. From the domestic circle, he can extend his thoughts over the whole field of society; going abroad into the living world, he can note its changes, and the laws by which they are governed; observing the throng of life, with the passions and interests that move its complicated mechanism, he will be able to unite comprehensive views with practical detail.

The study of man, as well as the love of man on the most ample scale, is a duty imposed on the preacher by the necessity of his office; and the more he is animated with the mind of Christ, the more faithful will he be to this duty, and the results of it will appear in his preaching, in the degree that he is earnest and sedulous in his Master's mission. Whatever there is in the love of universal man, that interests the philanthropist, and makes the world a common field of labor; whatever there is in love of country, that fans the fire of the patriot's breast; whatever there is in history, with all its grand and solemn exhibitions of the changeable, that feeds the meditations of senator or sage; whatever there is in the tendency of events, that occupies the speculative on the progression of humanity, are all tributary to the preacher, and in the highest, noblest sense. Upon the "field" of the world he is to sow imperishable seed; his patriotism must burn not with the heat of passion, but the glow of heaven; in

history he traces the path of Providence and the foot-
steps of God; and at the most distant limit to which
the reveries of earthly perfectionists extend, he stands
only on the margin of that infinite and immortal future,
which his faith discerns, and in which his faith confides.
The preacher has before him the whole range of nature; the visible and audible revelation of God, with
all the truth and piety which it contains and inspires.
The minister of the Creator ought surely to be familiar
with his works; and if there be any heart which they
can kindle with a pure enthusiasm, that heart ought to
be his.   The prophets, the great preachers of old, up-
lifted the soul through visible sublimity to the Eternal
Spirit; yet strange that religion, which in itself is highest poetry, should so often, in our modern pulpit, be
turned to meanest and tamest prose.

Ministers cannot be poets or prophets, but it is always
desirable they should be men of sensibility, men of
" natural piety."   An overloaded imagery, drawn from
external objects, we utterly denounce.   We wish not to
hear incessantly of suns, stars, skies, oceans, mountains, with their lofty sublimity; but we would have
the impression of a soul that had sympathy with greatness in any of the forms stamped by the hand of the
Almighty; we eschew all poetico-sentimental disserta-
tions in sermons upon fields and flowers, woods and

vales ; yet with the simplicity of taste and freshness of sentiment, which the love of such objects nourishes, we would not willingly dispense. We would not have prosaic moralizings on the change of seasons, but we look for that seriousness of thought and reflection, which proves that years have not passed in vain or unobserved ; and we cannot help thinking that, if such tastes were more cultivated, sermons would have more interest. But, above all, the preacher has the Bible, the household and holy book, the book of the affections, of the conscience, of faith and hope ; the book of childhood and of age, the guide of life and the consolation of death ; and from this treasury he can draw forth things old and new, which need but a living utterance to give them living power. We dwell not on the varied wisdom and sublimity of the Old Testament ; but in the New, not to enlarge on its boundless riches of narrative and precept, what mind or minds, what age or number of ages, will ever exhaust the moral meanings contained in the character of Christ ? and when will any individual or community ever translate into action the perfect lesson of his example ?

Whatever, therefore, may be drawn from man's history or destiny ; from feeling or from faith ; from imagination or memory ; from the heart, from the home, from the love of country or the love of man, from the universe or from the Bible, is fairly within the dominion of the pulpit. When we say this, we are not so unreasonable or so unjust as to imply that each single preacher should fill up the outline we have traced. Such a man would indeed be, what Charles the Second of England called Doctor Isaac Barrow, a most unfair preacher, for he would leave nobody else any thing to say. But if the pulpit has such manifold resources in the heart and conscience, in the domestic relations, in the outward world, in all that concerns man, past and future, how comes it then that our modern pulpit can possibly have the sameness of which we accuse it? Simply, because it has not used its resources; it has deserted the manifold revelations of God, and clung to the dogmas of theologians and system makers; it has forsaken the fountains of living waters, and hewn out for itself broken cisterns, which can hold no water. Is it any wonder, therefore, that the channels should be empty, and, that, where there should be the rush of healthful streams, there often are but echoes of hollow winds?

The second evil which we intimated in the modern pulpit, is its sectarianism, and to that point we now turn our attention. Looking at the question superficially, it would seem strange that the characteristic we have just discussed could possibly be joined with that which we have here stated. What in appearance can be so diverse, in many cases so opposed, as the Protestant sects ? How multifarious their names, and how fierce their controversies ! It might hence be concluded, that their opinions and their modes of illustration would be quite as diversified. It is possible, however, to have monotony of thought without unity of heart, and to be bound in the slavery of creeds, without being united in the bonds of charity ; it is, therefore, in no wise inconsistent, to hear parties rail at each other with all the Babel tongues of anger, although essentially they may be but little separated. Great differences make men serious ; it is commonly small differences that make them angry. The fiercest wars of the Liliputians were about breaking the big end or the little end of the egg. So it is that the sects fall out, not because they are far asunder, but because they are so near. But as the sober and thinking portions of mankind take no interest in these polemics, or merely stand by as cool spectators of the combat, to them the pulpit, while it assumes this aspect, can have neither attraction nor authority. We speak this not in scorn, but in sorrow ; for we know that fine minds and high talents are thus lost to the best hopes and interests of humanity, in beating the air and fighting with phantoms.

" Our theology," says Foster, the eloquent English essayist, " is the theology of faction." Few who have calmness and independence sufficient to judge the religious world as it is, will dispute the truth of this observation. In reference to the sectarian abuse of Christianity, it may indeed be truly said, that it "gives up to party what was made for mankind." In our modern pulpit there is little eloquence which speaks to the whole man. Rarely do we find — with regret we say it — a truthful, tranquil, loving administration of Christianity ; a going forth of great principles and great affections ; not the missiles of sectarian contest to be met by sectarian bulwarks, but the rays of that blessed light which melt the very barriers of ice, that would exclude them, into streams that spread life and splendor over a withered soil. Christianity is preached too commonly in a spirit of contention. We meet each other too often on those points at which we are antagonist ; as if the only prophecy of Jesus which we desired to fulfill, was that one in which he says, " I came not to send peace on earth, but a sword." We press the dogma of our sect, and we forget or forsake the spirit of our Master. Christian churches may literally use the saying of the great apostle, " Without are fightings, within are fears." It ought not so to be.

Whether as individuals or as churches, we require peace for our moral perfection, not the peace of apathy, but that of charity and toleration. Though occasionally conflict may be necessary to liberty, yet liberty itself is but a means to higher ends, and we value it for the happiness it promotes and secures. If all things great are sown in liberty, they are ripened in peace. Struggle may be necessary as a preliminary state; as a permanence it would be misery. The convulsion of disease may renovate the frame, and make returning health a rapture; but the rapture comes not until the convulsion subsides. Tempests may purify our atmosphere, but it is not until the storm and thunder are silent, and the fiery bolt shoots by, and the calm and sunshine come again, that we breathe with freedom, and look unfearing on the quiet face of nature. In the political and moral world the case is similar. The hurricane of a people's passions, generated in a people's wrongs, may shatter the thrones, that for a thousand years were based upon the wretchedness of successive millions, and supported by their tears and blood; yet the very shock that lays them in the dust, is for the time a calamity; and it is not until tranquillity returns, that freedom is known in its blessedness, and felt to be worth the sacrifice it cost. It is not until then its best effects are witnessed; that civilization lifts up a nation to virtue and grandeur, that industry spreads culture on its plains, and worships in safety under the vine and fig-tree it has planted. In religion, also, the ministries which expound its noblest sentiments, and carry out its best apostleship, must work in peace.

If it be said that Christ's religion has yet accomplished little compared with what might have been expected, the defect has been not in the spirit, but the forms with which it has been encumbered. The result of all is, that in this eternal attention to dogmatical distinctions, the intellect and heart of the minister are dwarfed, and the disciples are in the measure of their masters. While a few popular doctrines are continually reiterated, or points of dispute are urged with a zeal that often is but another name for bigotry, all that is serious in man's moral nature is left untouched ; a spurious excitement is mistaken for conversion, bodily impulses for sacred inspirations, and fierce denunciation of a different belief for holy ardor in the cause of Christ. The lovers of peaceful and thoughtful religion grieve ; the unbeliever sneers ; the intellectual retire to seek in their studies more congenial aliment, and from habitual, proceed to entire absence. The devotees applaud, but the great mass of society is left uninstructed in what they most need instruction, and unimproved in what they most need improvement. That a vast deal of our popular preaching is dogmatical or polemical, will not be denied by any person who is in the habit of hearing or reading our modern sermons ;

and often under the guise of religious phraseology there
is concealed a covert uncharitableness, which the advocate for Christ should blush to utter, which the disciples
of Christ should weep to hear.   In this our own country
of liberty, the most perfect religious freedom has not
entirely crushed religious asperity ; but what is wanting
in polemical rancor, we make up in fanatical extravagance.   But, bad as we may be in the warfare of
creeds, we thank Providence, that we are free at least
from the additional bitterness and burden of a church
establishment.

Yet we do not deprecate controversy, and we would
not banish argument from the pulpit ; for while men
think differently, — and think differently they will to
the end of the world, — controversy and argument
must exist by a necessity of our nature ; but, we
would have controversy tempered with charity, and
argument conducted with justice.   The polemical,
however, in any shape, is not that which should uni-
formly characterize discourses from the Christian
pulpit ; for although there is a time to pull down, as
to all things under the sun, there is a longer time and
a more arduous labor required to build up.   Let a
thoughtful man but take the New Testament in his
hand ; then contrast its spirit with the battlings of
Christendom, and he must lift up his eyes in wonder

or bend them down in shame. We may not feel this, because from familiarity we have lost our sensibility to the moral beauty of the Gospel, and habit has rendered our inconsistency imperceptible. But, as an example, suppose the case of a Mahommedan, who should feel aspirations after virtue higher than he knew, and had never seen a Christian, to find, in some stray leaf dropped from a traveller's Bible, " The Sermon on the Mount," how would his heart burn within him, how would he not say, " This is exactly the teaching that I want — how good and happy must those be who enjoy it!" Imagine him by circumstances thrown into a Christian land amidst the din of sects, where, instead of peace, and meekness, and purity of heart, he heard only the clashing of dogma against dogma, and the angry noise of mutual recrimination; it is probable that, as Luther returned from Rome a Protestant, he would leave Christendom more a Mahommedan than ever.

What are the prominent difficulties of the pulpit, is the most striking consideration that is suggested by the preceding observation. First, it has to meet the demands of a more diffused and a higher enlightenment. While the pulpit has been engaged in dogmatism or debate — a dogmatism, too, which was worn thread-bare two centuries ago, and debate that ought long since to have been at rest,—the press has been moulding the times, or going with them, and applying itself with hearty earnestness to whatever interests or raises man. We speak, as we before observed, of the better influences of the press. But, how, it may be inquired, does this concern the pulpit? Much every way; especially, inasmuch as it has to confront cultivated intellect instead of submissive faith. Education arouses anxieties unknown to the implicit devotee. In rendering men more deliberative, it renders them less susceptible; and while it weakens the powers of sense, it weakens also the sympathies of passion. Habitual thought restrains or conceals emotion, which by long constraint approaches to extinction. Artificial and refined habits of mind thus formed, often depress the devotional affections; the intellectual faculties outrun the religious, and study excludes faith.

Our times are those in which much is looked for from the men who have influence in the church or in the world. Much religious excitement prevails in our day, but the intellectual excitement is not less; and among those who are just awaking from the sleep of ignorance to a new existence, it has its deepest hold and most manifold dangers. The very eccentricities of intellect, the vagaries and paradoxes of recent speculation, surround the pulpit with new and fresh difficulties.

The dangers that arise from intellect alone, the pulpit but rarely or ineffectually meets. It has declaimed on the delusions of imagination and the wildness of passion; but it should now be prepared, not only to meet the demands of reason, but to obviate its dangers. The Christian ministry has given a disproportionate attention to the sins and sufferings of passion, but sins and sufferings are also connected with intellect, and these are equally within its scope of influence and sphere of duty. The ministration therefore of the pulpit becomes more arduous with the spread of reading; and though the audience should consist merely of unwashed artificers, preachers must not calculate on uninquiring deference, nor imagine they need but a small amount of mental exertion, to satisfy persons, whose grade of information they would judge by their grade in life. In such inference they will find themselves fatally mistaken.

The pulpit, in emulation with the good agency of the press, must stand at enmity with the bad. We revere the press as much as any lovers of freedom and knowledge can venerate that which is their great palladium. We are aware that, even in its periodical form, it has been the medium of giving to the world some of the most beautiful productions of genius; but we are also aware, that, in its inferior grades, it has been the pander to every bad and gross passion ; to envy, hatred, malice, revenge, and licentiousness : for profit, setting honor, truth, and conscience at defiance ; praising or blaming not according to justice, but according to faction ; always ready to be bought or bribed ; at all hours prepared with a dagger and a masque, which may as easily be had for hire as those of Italian bravoes.

That no pen worth using could be turned to such vile purposes, it is sincerely to be hoped ; for of all species of degradation, this hiring of the mind to falsify for pelf all its better sentiments, is the basest and the worst. If a man, who had ever any thing nobler in his nature, should by wretchedness be driven to such mean offices as a refuge from starvation, then we say that poverty has poured out upon his head her last and her most bitter vial. That such publications exist here and in Europe, publications which shrink from no species of venal corruption, from no vileness of mental dishonesty ; whose very life is slander, whose breath is obscene and contaminated, we lament to confess in a Christian and a civilized country. And the circulation of these is principally among the lower grades of the operative classes. The injury they have done, in misleading opinion and debasing morals, is one of the most awful social evils, and of all abuses of the press the most to be deplored. The difficulty, then, of the pulpit in this respect is twofold ; namely, to keep pace with the intelligence of the higher press, and to subdue the corruption of the lower.

Secondly. Our age is one of vast materiality and vast excitement ; an age of mechanism and agitation. The powers that work around us are impressive and gigantic. By the agency of steam alone, more is accomplished than was ever painted in the wildest fictions which charmed our childhood. Oceans are made as ferries ; extremes of continents as places of immediate neighborhood ; one central force can keep thousands in motion ; a man with a dirty jacket, sitting on the engine of a railway train, turns into contempt all our childish imaginations of the giant with his seven-leagued boots. What was fiction to our grandfathers, is commonplace to us ; what to them would have been a wild and airy dream, is to us a real and substantial fact. The astonishing progress of material activity and mechanical invention, has dispersed the visions of enthusiasm by which we were once encompassed. The colored lamp in which the light was placed, that gave a thousand hues and figures to our sight, is broken ; the hues and figures have vanished with the broken lamp, and to advanced experience the naked lustre alone remains. The world's youth seems past. Hitherto, it has dreamed and fancied, imagined and reflected ; now it is to work ;

philosophy and poetry are daily issuing into action, and science is discarding soul.

When we speak of science thus, we mean that which is now most prevalent, the science of things limited and tangible. In these we have, no doubt, amazing agencies, majestic to the senses, and even sublime to thought; but still they are all material, and form a bottomless gulph, in which the individualities of mind are buried by millions. Evidence there may be of profound intellect in the originator, but it is intellect operating through material media, and using the men whom it employs, not so much as thinking beings as the adjuncts of machinery. The direct tendency is to reduce all skilled industry to monotonous uniformity, and to render successive millions of human beings the automatons of mechanistic despotism. Habits generated from influences like these, are the most remote from those which it is the office of the pulpit to instil; a sense of inward existence, of a spirit superior to the outward and the perishable, and of a free and responsible will.

We have said that our age is one of excitement; and such it is for religion, politics, and wealth. We have in the religious world whole forests of societies, with so many cross-paths and so much intricacy, that simple piety and philanthropy become bewildered in their mazes. We have, also, so many preachers, at least in our towns, so quick a succession of services, and so continual an administration of religious stimulants, that the head grows giddy, and one sermon stifles another. We stop not here to descant on excitement in politics ; for since the building of Babel, politics have been clamorous with a many-tongued confusion; on this point, we cannot single out one age from another. The passion for power is universal and indestructible, from the statesman, that by a magnificent genius rules half a world, to the pot-house factionist, that by strength of lungs drowns the vociferations of a club. But wealth has never been pursued with a more absorbing desire, than in the present age ; yet the pursuit is not so much in a hoarding spirit, as in a passionate enthusiasm. Ambition, vanity, emulation ; artificial wants, created by artificial life ; a false standard of competence, and an idea of happiness still more false, urge men onward in this career with an intensity that engrosses every faculty and fills the whole life with care.

Our age, moreover, so far as it is not fanatical, is one of skepticism ; and by skepticism, we do not mean merely what is implied in conventional phraseology, — an outward disregard to religious institutions, nor even professed disbelief in the doctrines of Christianity. It is not the philosophical skepticism of Hume, which destroying all grounds of conviction, in its very extreme carried its own cure. That which admits of no certainty in any form of evidence leaves all evidence as it had been. The reasonings of Hume had no force even to himself out of his closet ; they could never have influence on the opinions of mankind, and to the philosophical they can be only subjects of metaphysical amusement. Nor is our skepticism like that of Voltaire, one of wit and scorn, joining sarcasm with ridicule, and in place of direct logic using the sting of insinuation. Ours is a skepticism, that, though less defined, lies deeper and is more dangerous ; a skepticism, not so much in opinion as in sentiment ; not so much the skepticism of criticism as of indifference. The material world so presses us on every side, and an immediate utility is so interwoven with our actions and philosophy, that all else appear nonentities. We are as the disciple Thomas ; we must see with our eyes and touch with our hands, or we will not be convinced ; and what we see and touch must have some alliance with our interest, to be for us of any value or importance.

Our Saviour said, " Blessed are those who have not seen and yet believe ; " blessed, also, and blessed above measure; are those who understand the full import of that saying. The faith of the heart has waxed cold, the ears are dull of hearing ; and a hard and rigid

matter-of-fact philosophy has grown upon us, in which
the divine and the ideal are never dreamt of.   Thence,
the past, the distant, and the future, by apprehension of
which, as Doctor Johnson taught, we rise in the scale
of intelligent beings, have lost their power on us ; and
thence also disinterested actions, and a sense of right
which defies consequences come to be regarded as the
mere dreams of amiable enthusiasts.   From such rea-
soners the progressive capacities of human nature meet
with equal mockery, and with its capacities depart its
claims.   Incessant contact with the actual has blunted
our perception of the ideal ; that moral imagination has
grown insensible, which reveals to our souls the pure
and beautiful, whether in the divine character or the
human ; in the actions of men or in the works of the
Creator.   The faith of sympathy, by which we realize
all that is not palpable, has weakened into feebleness,
and in the same proportion have our reverence and
admiration.

It is not that the faculties are destroyed ; but they
slumber.   The faculties which bind man to the invisible
cannot be destroyed ; they are stronger than those
which unite him to the visible ; the one shall perish, the
others remain forever.   And there is no man, however
low or brutish, who does not on occasions feel this in
his own experience ; — occasions, when the strongest

shrink at the idea of death and judgment; when the hero forgets his glory and the miser forgets his gain. Sunk we may be in the very depths of materiality, yet times there are, of sober reflections and visitings of thought, that make us sadder as they make us wiser, when we cannot shut out unseen things, nor even subdue our desire for them; times when we feel that the wishes which were as fire in our breast were but delusions, the love of glory a splendid falsehood, and outward advantages without inward peace but the mockeries of our wretchedness; times when we learn the emptiness of riches, the vanities of rank, the dependency of power, the burden of fame, the changes of life — the uncertainty of all. Then we look for other objects of desire; our ideas rise from sense to faith, from the seen to the unseen, from the house of clay to the temple of the Eternal; feeling that passion sinks as we wane in life; that the brilliancy of earth fades the more we gaze upon it; that mutability attends all with which we are here connected; we long at last for something beyond the passions, time, and change; something of which no vicissitude in this world can rob us, which we can have or hope for, though the eye should lose its sight and the ear its hearing, though riches should be no more, and earthly expectations blasted forever. Then we turn to God who cannot alter, and to a future world which cannot end. But, although the tendencies that impel us thus to look beyond the space we live in are inherent and indestructible, there are periods unfavorable to their exercise; and such a one is the present. There is a moral as well as theological skepticism; our times are those of moral skepticism. Popular odium is principally directed against the theological unbeliever, but the skeptic of the heart is infinitely the worse. One may believe theologically, even to superstition, yet be morally a skeptic, — a skeptic to all that is good, fair, generous, and great; one may doubt because he cannot help it, yet have faith unconquerable in everlasting truth and goodness.

To make our distinction a little more clear, we will adduce for each part of it a single illustration. Louis the Fourteenth, it is well known, was in the close of his life as stanch a devotee, as he had ever been an inveterate persecutor. He was, it is true, not the right-minded believer, but he was no skeptic, and this is all our argument requires. Take then the following anecdote of him. " Marechal, his surgeon, observing him unusually melancholy, ventured to hint some fears of his health. The monarch acknowledged, in general terms, that he suffered great uneasiness from the posture of his affairs. Eight or ten days after, having recovered his ordinary tranquillity, he sent for Mare-chal,. and, taking him aside — 'Now' said he, 'that I feel myself at ease, I will relate to you the cause of my anxiety, and by what means I got rid of it.' He proceeded to inform him, that the necessity of his affairs having compelled him to impose new taxes on his people, his reluctance to make free with their pro-perty, and his compassion for their distress, had greatly affected him. 'At length,' said he, 'I opened my mind to Father Tellier, who required some days to consider on the subject. He has now brought me a consultation of the most subtle doctors of Sorbonne, who all agree, that as the whole property of my subjects is personally mine, I can take nothing from them but what is my own. This decision has restored me to the tranquillity I had lost.' " We see here how far a man can be credulous and cruel ; or rather, we see how easily a devout casuist can suit his faith to his practice and his passions. Contrast with this the case of Madame Roland, unbeliever as she was, strong in the faith of rectitude and humanity, maintaining that faith in the midst of tyrants and on the bloody scaffold. Put, then, the theological unbelief of the heroic woman against the moral unbelief of the superstitious despot, and our distinction will be at once apprehended. Skepticism on great truths we deplore in any shape ; but if we had the power of choice we would say, " at all events," keep the moral nature trustful and pure, and the wanderings of judgment may be corrected by the experience of the heart, and, in time, right sentiment may produce right belief.

We have thus, briefly as we could, stated a few of the difficulties with which, in the present day, the pulpit has to contend. The pulpit is the great expositor of religion, and as religion is an essential element in human nature it can never be extinguished. The duty, therefore, which it cannot desert, it must gird on strength to accomplish. The pulpit has a solemn position and a solemn duty, a duty, not to sect, but to society, and not alone to society but to the world, and to the world in all its grandest relations. In what spirit, then, must it go to this noble and glorious work ? It must take with it a human and kindly Christianity, and peace and good will must be its message. It must not have a creed in one hand and a thunderbolt in the other ; but it must rather take the hymn in which a Saviour's birth was sung, and the cross on which a Saviour's love was proved. It must have freedom, but it must not have harshness and prejudice : it must be as the mercy it proclaims, impartial and unconfined; like the sun-lit dew by which that mercy is figured, falling on the most retired and lowly spots, and coming from a bright and all-embracing heaven. It must have power, and power sanctified; a power great in its very rest, which, like Elijah's prayer, cleaves the skies and draws down fire from above.

We can easily discern what should be the spirit of the pulpit; we cannot so easily specify what should be its form. Young men, preparing for the ministry, used once to be directed to the classic age of the French church for models of pulpit oratory; but such a custom is far better broken than observed. Many of the French preachers were supreme in thought and utterance, for their own times and for their own purposes. Their productions live in the literature of the world, and will live while the world has a literature.

All oratory must be suited to its age and to its auditories. The eloquence of Bossuet, lofty and massive at it was, would not have melted, as Whitefield's did, the miners of Cornwall; nor would the sentiments of Fenelon, with his silvery elocution, have fallen with the same power on an English multitude as the shrill declamation of Wesley. Though we were able to call from the dead Bourdaloue, serious, logical, cold, and clear; or Massillon, full of fervor and pathos; we cannot bring back their age, their church, their ceremonies, and their congregations. The solemn mass, the deep-toned choir, the courtly audience, the lofty pillars, and the fretted aisles, were all proper concomitants of their eloquence ; but that is not the eloquence which we most need. They discoursed before the satiated and voluptuous on the sinfulness of worldly pleasures ; our ministers are more frequently called on to give a solace for worldly pains. They, speaking to those who were gorged with all they could desire in life, threw an awful terror around the bed of death ; but our preachers speak to numbers who have not had life in its fullness but its wants, and for whom there is no brightness if it rest not on the grave. They addressed an ambitious aristocracy on the vanity of earthly glory ; it is more frequently the duty of our ministers to elevate men to a sense of their heavenly and human dignity. They discoursed on life and death ; and though on both they discoursed most eloquent music, much of their declamation was false in spirit and false in fact.

What then is the kind of preaching likely to suit the times, to meet the wants and requirements of the age ? In a few words we shall say what it must not be. It must not be a dull enunciation called " rational ; " nor cold disquisition denominated " ethical ; " nor a textual compound without connection or unity, dignified with the epithet of " Scriptural." We cannot accept for a Christian sermon a composition, wanting in all that a Christian sermon ought to have, warmth, energy, tenderness, pathos, elevation of thought and spirituality of sentiment.

We have already said sufficient to show the necessity of cultivated intellect in preaching; but more is still needed, as may be seen by a glance at the difficulties we have enumerated. The pulpit must become more adaptive. We use a new word, but we have no other that so well defines our idea. It is the great beauty of the Gospel, as it was of Christ's own personal ministry, that it suits every age and every class. Christ instructed all, and in every place; the priest, the scribe, the fisherman, the sinful woman and the pure; in the temple, in the market-place, in the dwelling, along the highway, on the hill-side, by the well; and his preaching was always modified according to character and circumstances. So should ever be the administration of his religion. Christianity is not a set of hard and dry propositions, but a vital and diffusive spirit, which can mingle with the whole moral life, and sanctify it in every action. In these days, preaching must diversify its topics, and widen the field of its ministry. Instead of dogmas, it must take principles; principles it must apply to practice; and practice implies the whole character and conduct of man in all his relations, personal, domestic, and public. Abstractions and theories in religion do not touch the heart or reform the life.

We must, therefore, be made to feel that religion is our highest interest, by intimate and vivid associations. Active and thinking men seek in the pulpit what they desire every where, simplicity and earnestness; but exaggeration they despise and avoid.

Now, it unfortunately happens, that exaggeration is the great sin of our modern preachers. In most of their declamatory descriptions, the world and all things therein, are evil and accursed; a pall is on the heavens, and darkness on the earth; and but a favored few are saved from this present and prospective hell. States of feeling, the most sickly and unsound, are given as religious sentiment, and appeals made to the pious, which can only tend to nourish the most egregious self-conceit. Persons, who know the world and human nature as they are, grow disgusted with all this; and the men who utter it, they cannot help thinking fools or hypocrites. They are well aware that earth is not a Paradise, but they are equally sure that it is not a Pandemonium; they are conscious that humanity is not perfect, but they will not believe the rhapsodies which would make it appear Satanic. Truth, then, must be adhered to in descriptions of experience, as well as in statements of principles; in experience above all, for the hearer has the test within himself, and if he finds that stated as a certainty, which is false to his entire consciousness, and remote from all his associations, he loses trust in the speaker, and perhaps makes shipwreck of his faith. If men are worldly, the more need to convince them that religion has a substantial existence ; if ardent, to breathe a pure inspiration into their enthusiasm ; if skeptical, to display with more force the reality and grandeur of Christ's character ; and it is required that these principles should be pressed on men in connection with their habitual feelings and pursuits.

Morality, as commonly taught in the pulpit, is the most vague of generalities ; having neither distinctness of analysis nor force of application. Preaching, without losing elevation or spirituality, should assume more directness ; meet the mechanic at his bench, the trader at his desk, and all according to their several positions and obligations. Preachers must not take for granted that, because the principles of duty are uniform and unchangeable, all men, therefore, view right and wrong through the same medium, or judge them by the same standard. There is a conventional morality, with which most persons satisfy the world and their conscience ; they are not worse than others in their trade or profession, and they all have common cause not to be too critical or uncharitable. A sophistry of this kind, which eats away the very life of virtue, can never be successfully combated in the pulpit, except by an application to the details of life, that is as searching as it is accurate ; and while we would have preaching become thus intelligibly practical, we neither secularize nor degrade it. We do not desire from the pulpit a lecture on metaphysics, a dissertation on political economy, or a harangue on daily politics ; but we would have that from it for which Christianity was intended, counsel in all our difficulties, and guidance in all our duties. Preachers, as they arise, should be trained for the age in which they are to labor. We cannot frequently have genius, but we may hope for zeal and nature ; we may not look for a dazzling eloquence, but we may, for what is better and more effective, moral power flowing from moral sympathy, which, if it does not create the classic oratory that is immortalized on earth, trains the sainted virtue that ascends to Heaven. We ask not for men to arouse a world, but we despair not of those who can sanctify a church. We hope for men to arise and multiply, who shall come armed for the temper of the times ; who shall come moulded, but not corrupted, by the influences amidst which they live ; imbued with the religion they are to administer, an earnest and awakening Christianity ; who shall come with that practical sagacity, which, joined with high sentiment, rises into wisdom; who shall come with right knowledge quickened by right enthusiasm, with the fire which is enkindled in the sanctuary, that warms and fertilizes while it enlightens and beautifies.

But when the pulpit has done all it can do, and done it in the best manner, there are still many in moral destitution whom it cannot reach. The energetic benevolence of modern times has made efforts to meet this great spiritual want, in the establishment of city missions and of the ministries at large. As to the need of them, it is only to be wondered it was not sooner felt; but even late, we hail this establishment. We lament, in our common religious phraseology, the sin and misery of past times and of distant nations; we multiplied missionaries, and we accumulated funds to carry the Gospel to the extremities of the earth, but we seemed to forget that as great sin and misery were at our doors; and while we wailed over the wretchedness of the heathen, we thought not that only a brick wall, perhaps, stood between us and crime, as deep as ever the olden ages knew, and misery as great as lowest savages endure. The secluded lane was morally as unknown to the grand street behind which it stood, as a nook in the interior of Africa; and a groan in the one perished as unheard and as unnoticed as a groan in

the other.   Without the form, there existed in the dark
retreats of the civilized world all the abominations of
idolatry; and without the dedication of temples to vile
and evil demons, there was, in the hidden places of
poverty and crime, a multitude of victims to the worst
principles which their names embodied.   The domestic
ministry has done much to break down these partitions,
which kept one half the world ignorant about the condition of the other; it has entered the dens of neglected
vice and desolation, and made revelations on the state
of the poor and the forsaken, of which " good, easy "
people had never dreamt.   Without crossing oceans to
Africa, Hindostan, or New Zealand, it has found in our
own cities a terra incognita of manifold ignorance,
crime, and sorrow; and while men's sympathies were
wafting to the poles, it has recalled them to their
thresholds.   May it continue to go forward and increase,
for there is yet a mighty work to be accomplished, and
blessed indeed are the laborers, who shall be called to
it, and who shall be found worthy of it.   Of all ministries, it is that which most resembles Christ's; which
goes to men's homes and to their hearts; which looks
for the wretched and the lost, and which not merely
calls but seeks; of all ministries, it is that which requires most of Christ's spirit, and which, divested of all
declamatory pomp, must go at once to the soul in the

strong persuasiveness of a true and sympathizing humanity.

Domestic missions are not yet as numerous as they might be, and as they will be ; but so far as they have gone, there is abundance of reason to look gratefully on the origin of the institution, and to hope largely for the future. Already they have done good beyond calculation, and our hope is high, when we think of what they are destined to fulfill. How many, in the last wretchedness of despair, have been found out in their sunless lairs ; how many, in the pangs of unhoping poverty, in the madness of forlorn ruin ; how many, in starving and houseless sin, outcast from the good, and with no pity from those as bad as themselves ; how many, in the pangs of death, who long for consolation as the hart for the water brooks ; how many of the virtuous sitting low in uncomplaining resignation ; how many of all these have been discovered in the wilderness of modern society by researches of domestic ministers, who brought light to their dwellings, and salvation to their souls ; confidence to the weak in heart, and strength to those who were ready to perish ? Christ's spirit and Christ's peace be on their labors ! To these we may add a great mass of voluntary preachers, as distinguished from the regular and settled ministry. Both on this side and the other of the Atlantic, very many congregations could not afford to support a pastor, and therefore necessity, made more urgent by piety, compels them to arrange the services among themselves; and those who are most competent, lead the devotions of the others. Congregations we know, who have thus grown up strong in faith and virtue, and progressive in numbers and in power; men, humble men, but honest; men of lowly rank, but eloquent with the force which truth and sincerity inspire, have become hoary as their unpaid teachers; working with their hands, and among their fellows during the week, but standing first and most revered among them on the Sabbath; and without either crosier or mitre, they have never failed to receive that veneration, which is always willingly given to the pure and single-hearted. And what a noble honor is theirs! men, who, after their six days' toil, can, on the seventh, disenthral themselves from earth, pass from the laborer to the pastor, minister to their brethren the glories of an upper world, point to brighter worlds, and lead the way; men, who in simplicity, fervor, and success, do an apostle's office with an apostle's disinterestedness.

In conclusion, we look on to the future confidingly. With a press free and diffusive; with a literature growing cheap as it becomes more elevated; with increasing facilities in the fine arts, to habituate the sight of all classes to forms of grace and beauty, and tune their ears to the music of sweet sounds ; with the spread of a peaceful and moral civilization, and a widening community by means of science and commerce ; with education in Sunday and week schools, enlarging in domain as it is improving its methods, we trust, also, to see the pulpit honorably fill its own place in the grand work of moral redemption and moral progression.

PATRIOTISM.

I WILL enter into no metaphysical inquiries on the origin and nature of this sentiment. We have no time for such preliminary disquisition. I will, in the first place, consider it simply in itself. In the second place, I will refer to some erroneous feelings often associated with it. In conclusion, I will dwell on its positive and undeniable obligations.

And, first, in itself, this indeed needs no recondite examination. That an attachment exists in our nature to the place of our birth, and by association to the country which contains it, is a proposition which logic cannot aid; for, if we do not feel it, it is a proposition of which there is no reasoning to convince us. It admits of no contradiction, or being contradicted, there is no process of thought, by which it can be proved. It is not a sentiment that springs up with instruction; on the contrary, it dates back before all training, and centres in those affections, of which, even the individual memory holds no records of the beginning. It is not a local distinction. With degrees and differences, it is found wherever man is found. It is of no particular age, and of no specific culture. There are no traditions without its inspiration; there are no traditions in which it is not the most stirring story; there is no song, however early, or however rude, of which it is not the boldest poetry, in which it is not the most soul-enkindled and the most soul-enkindling music. It lives in all civilization, it lives before any; it begins before comparison, and it survives all calculation. A man does not love the country of his birth, because it is more beautiful than another; because it is more fertile; because it is more prosperous; because it has more knowledge and more power; because it gives him more to enjoy, and less to suffer. Men will hold, with the almost tenacity of affection, to countries the most unsightly, the most unpicturesque, and the most unlovely; they will cling to regions barren and inclement, ay, and love them just as fondly, as if they were vales in Araby the blest, or the fairest spots in the fairest districts of Italy. Who has not heard of northern savages returning to their lairs in the snow, and of American Indians rushing again from all the luxuries of civilization, to their wigwams in the wilderness? Have not civilized men, too, from the midst of knowledge, liberty, and peace, turned back the gaze of their hearts over years and distance, resting with unspeakable delight upon regions which gave them nothing, but a hungry childhood and a neglected youth ? And such is the charm of imagination, that these regions, seen through the dimness of time, are invested with a mystic beauty, which nothing but the most hallowed instincts could shed around them.

Is not this well ? Such facts give all the reply, which should ever be attempted, to mean or narrow theories of our nature. They show that there is a spirit within, whose workings are not the mere agency of sense. There is nothing in mere sensation which tells me, why I love a stunted shrub in one climate, more than fragrant bowers in another. I give myself, therefore, to the conviction, that it is something in me which passeth sense. Nor shall I be persuaded in the face of these facts, that whatever feeling in man becomes a motive, and whatever motive in him becomes an action, can always be accounted for on the ground of selfishness. Assertions so vague, and so indiscriminate, would include, under one broad generalization, states of mind and forms of conduct, the most abhorrent of each other, and the most opposed. If, merely, the respect to self decided the human will, then actions would be traced to the same principle, and ascribed to the same spirit, however contradictory in the doing; there would be no difference between them, but that of sagacity or obtuseness, of rashness or of prudence — in a word, of accurate or inaccurate calculation; moral distinctions would be at an end; and as to the object, the aim, and purpose of the deed, we must place within the same classification, the man who sells his life for his country, and the man who sells his country for his life.

But, it is in this, as it is in every thing which pertains to our higher being, no theory can grasp or comprehend it. Even the beauty of which the senses take account, the senses cannot explain; how much beyond them, then, is that beauty which the soul creates to the soul, a beauty with which the senses have no concern! There is emotion which brings to self, profound enjoyment, in which the good of self had never been contemplated. There is reality which evades all definitions; there is truth beyond the reach of logic; there is a worth, which no standard of external utility can estimate or measure. That tendency in our nature to idealize the country of our affections, which clothes an uncouth edifice with glory; which causes the sight of a treeless mountain to stir the heart like the sound of a trumpet; which moves us to weeping by the hearing of a rustic tune; that tendency, I say, has this utility, has this truth, has this worth; and although the truth is beyond the record of logic; although the worth is no subject for arithmetical calculation; although the reality admits of no tangible admeasurement, the tendency explains itself by all that gives eloquence to history, and justifies itself by all that gives heroism to action.

This sentiment, like every other, is subject, of course, to great variety of modification, according to individual character, general culture, religious systems, and political institutions. The inhabitants of mountainous regions have been especially remarked for the force of their attachment to their native districts. How is this to be explained? Is it by the nature of the outward scenery, or by the influences of the social condition? If we allude only to outward scenery, is it that the bold distinctness, the picturesque relief of the landscape, entwine themselves more with the feelings, and lay a more tenacious hold upon the memory, than spaces of orderly uniformity, or of quiet beauty? Is it that the pointed crag, the dizzy precipice, the chasms that seem yawning to the centre, the summits that stretch above the mid-air clouds, the valleys that sink into nether darkness? Is it that such pungent, such strongly expressed forms of external phenomena, strike more deeply into the life, and grapple on its thoughts with indestructible recollections? Is it that the gurgling murmur of the torrent, the mighty harmony of the cataract, the symphonies of winds among the glens, the stupendous thunderings of storms amidst the mountains; the choruses of tempestuous echoes, rolling through the caves, softening by distance into plaintive sweetness, and coming to fancy as the still small voice of spirits far away; voices that create, forever, sweet music in the heart, and which only ceases, when the chords of being are unstrung? Is it, likewise, that amidst the loneliness of hills, there is more meditation, and that there is more self-communion? Is it, that by these means, there is a deeper experience of the individual existence, and of the hidden life? And is it that, by such association, there grows up a more intimate connection with the external objects linked to it? Is it, too, that, in mountainous districts, there is a life of buoyancy, of boldness, of adventure, of risks encountered and escaped, of perils never to be forgotten, of achievements, always to be proud of? Is it that when things are thus woven into feeling, men love them for the dangers that are past? Is it, moreover, that, in such districts, from paucity of inhabitants, the residents become attached, not only by the power of the local instinct, but still more strongly by the ties of kindred?

There is something, no doubt, in the character of

outward nature as thus developed, to bind the heart to certain localities, and also, there is much in the social conditions which they originate and sustain ; but to enter fully into these points, would lead us farther than at present we can go. I think that, as a mere fact, that mountaineers have a more passionate local patriotism than other men, and we will content ourselves with the conviction, that the external scenery, and the social life trained up amidst such regions, both contribute in adding to the strength of the emotion. As the same influences render them healthy, hardy, elastic, impulsive, and impassioned, they render them, also, tenacious of local habits and traditions, impatient of restraint, and lovers of their own ways and their own will. Jealous of their local privileges, they have always been the most determined maintainers of national independence, and the most courageous antagonists to foreign jurisdiction. Illustrations need not be adduced, because every child's memory is filled with them ; for, what child, that has learned any thing, does not know the ancient bravery of hilly Greece, and the modern sturdiness of Alpine Switzerland ?

And above all, Palestine ! Palestine of mountains ! What child does not remember Judea amongst the hills ? There it was the patriarchs mused ; there it was they tended their flocks ; there it was that Abraham, Father of the faithful, sat in the door of his tent, and called strangers to its shelter, entertaining angels unawares; there it was, that Jacob died; from thence, was Joseph sold; thither was Moses with his great army commissioned to return. Upon those hills did judges wander, whose laws have filled the world; upon those hills, kings were nurtured, whose glory will never die; amidst those valleys, prophets slept, whose dreams, visions, and utterance, transcend all the philosophy that men have spoken. There sprung up mighty and royal men, with quenchless national faith, and pure national enthusiasm; having, in the line of its history, Moses, who spoke with God, David who gave to earth the music of heaven, and the Maccabees, who enriching the soil which they defended with their blood, consecrated its history, everlastingly, with their memories. Thence it was that Jesus sprung, with that measureless heart of his, that, clasping all the human family in its generous regard, had yet tears of bitter sorrow to pour over the devoted towers of Jerusalem. And there it was that Paul arose, the eloquent Apostle of the Gentiles, whose bosom, filled with the most majestic Christian philanthropy, turned with a bleeding affliction to seek for the sympathy of his countrymen. And, long through the course of centuries scattered over the world; immersed in every gain-seeking employment, the children of Abraham are dispersed ; still, the hills and valleys, where Abraham fed his flocks, are dearer to them than the jewels which the richest of his posterity have collected, than the gold which the proudest of them have gathered ; and the most indigent would rather dwell securely in the tabernacles of ancient Israel, than in the most gorgeous and marble palaces of modern kings.

Patriotism does not when strongest, as an instinct, show itself in its largest nobility ; in a rude time, it does not display itself in its grandest characteristics. In such circumstances it is wanting in compass of moral aspiration ; but then it makes up for this want, in the intensity of its generous devotion, and of its individual loyalty. Many, while I speak, will call to mind an eloquent passage in " The Fair Maid of Perth," in which Sir Walter Scott describes a battle in the Scottish highlands between two rival clans, where an old man sacrifices the lives of his six sons and then his own, to defend the person of his chieftain, and to conceal his cowardice. This, it may be said, is fiction, still it is nature. I will, then, give a passage from history which I met in one of the reviews, concerning a wild tribe of the highlands, called the clan Chattan. " Two hundred of them were, on a certain occasion, captured by the earl of Moray, and hanged. But their head, Hector

Macintosh, lay concealed, and there was the most ardent desire, on the part of the captors, to apprehend him. Not one of all the two hundred could be induced to confess where Hector was, though life was severally offered to them on this condition, as each was led to the gallows. Their faith was so true, that they could not be persuaded, either by fair means or by any terror of death, to betray their captain."

Patriotism of a high order must grow out of a wider culture, and be connected with a civilization in which such a culture can be developed. This culture involves some of the grandest moral principles, and the purest social aims; and in very rude conditions, these moral principles are not discerned, and these social aims are not conceived. The original desire, that of loyalty to our nation, is, to be sure, the essence of patriotism, and to this, the patriotism of a New-Zealand savage may be as true as the patriotism of a Roman citizen. The love of our country in the lowest state is a noble emotion, a concentration of the most liberal and the most refined affections; the love of home, the love of kindred; the love of the past, and the love of posterity.

But the love of our country, however strong as I have said, as a rude instinct, is not great. Patriotism is great, only as an enlightened principle; and it becomes an enlightened principle only, by the advancement of social and moral cultivation.   By such cultivation alone, the real greatness and happiness of a country are dis- cerned ; for, in what do the real greatness and happi- ness of a nation centre ?   Not in physical prosperity ; not in the arts, either, which embellish luxury ; not even in the richest literature or the loftiest science.   These are not unworthy of regard ; but a nation may have them all, and yet be unsound or dying.   The true greatness and the true happiness of a country consist in wisdom ; in that enlarged and comprehensive wisdom, which includes education, knowledge, religion, virtue, freedom ; with every influence which advances, and every institution which supports them.   The idea of such happiness and such greatness can have no ade- quate nourishment, but in civilized society ; and it is only the best even in that society who are true to the idea.   The man of base or selfish passions, the man of narrow or bigoted understanding, is not capable of a true patriot's expansion.

Not such were the men who live in the deathless affections of their respective nations.   They were men of exalted moral beauty ; the prophets and the apostles to millions ; the sages who taught multitudes lessons of immortal freedom ; the exemplars, who set before them models of heroic excellence ; the martyr-confessors who sealed those lessons by their death ; or the triumphant conquerors, who confirmed them by their victory; the Andrew Marvells, the Franklins, the Hampdens, the Sydneys, the Kosciuskoes, the Emmetts of the world. The name of Washington, I mention singly and alone. It admits of no plural or parallel. The grand one who bore it comes to our thoughts without comparison, and without companion. In his own majestic individuality, he stands separate from the crowd of warriors, yet he is close to the hearts of his species; they give him a love which no other soldier has excited, and they approach him with a homage which no other soldier has deserved.

Men, such as these, were not the men that could have arisen on a savage age; they were not the minds which gross or barbarous times could have educated; they were not the minds which gross or barbarous objects could have excited. They were men consecrated for a mighty work; and the states of society which called them forth, they, in their turn, contributed to advance. They were men, who could stand before any tribunal by which the purest state of society could try them. There was nothing in their lives that sought disguise, or that feared an accusation; they had no cunning which they would cover with the robe of wisdom; there were no dark spots upon their character, which needed the bloody shroud of the scaffold or the battle to conceal; no blotches lay upon their names, which could only be scorched out by the death-baptism of a fiery persecution; independent for their essential greatness on misfortune or success, those for whom they died could add nothing to the goodness which gave their dying lustre, or those to whom they imparted freedom could shed no glory on the boldness which achieved it. They were men of large discourse, of wide relations; and though they were men of immovable convictions and of dauntless zeal, they were men of many-sided tolerance; men in whom the devotion to exalted principles, was so combined with energetic personality, that, in respecting themselves, they respected others; admired the independence in others which for themselves they claimed; demanded no liberty for themselves which they did not demand for all; asserted that such liberty belonged to inalienable rights, and held that inalienable rights were the property of man. Inconsistencies, indeed, there may have been, doubtless there were, between their conduct and their ideas; but still, the direction of their conduct was ever, on the whole, guided by their ideas, and if they did not always reach the perfect right, they kept their faces towards it.

Great patriots, therefore, must be men of great excellence; and it is this alone that can secure to them a lasting admiration. It is by this alone, that they become noble to our memories, and that we feel proud in the privilege of doing reverence to their nobleness. Great names stand not alone for great deeds; they stand also for great virtues, and in doing them worship, we elevate ourselves. In our gratitude we simply evince our sensibility to excellence, and show that we can be affected by it. Great names raise us from our own dead level of worldliness by their generous aspirations; they wrench us from the bondages of self into the open scope of their own free souls, and we have to thank them, not only for an improved social condition, but for a more exalted inward existence. Such names are the truest and the most genuine wealth any nation can possess, and the more she has of them, the more abundant are her treasures. They are incomparably of higher value, than richest argosies on the sea, or than mines of the finest gems within the land; they are, too, the most enduring wealth. Time, which deteriorates other possessions, adds preciousness to those; time, which defaces or obscures the fairest things, dissolves the mists which, for a little, overshadow glorious names; gradually, the shadows pass away, and they come out with undimmed effulgence to the clearest eye of distant generations. When cities decay; when commerce changes its markets and its highways; when buildings, once of proudest structure, are antiquated or in ruins; when laws and institutions, customs and traditions, have undergone all possible vicissitudes of reversal; the great and the good names of a nation are still within it, a priceless inheritance; and that inheritance it cannot forfeit, except by an apostasy which renders it incapable of holding it, or unworthy of the claim. They are living wealth. They constitute the vitality of the ages to which they pertain, and they send vitality down to ages which come long after. There is a power in their sound, which, at times, can quicken the dust and the clods; the dead in the graves of their slavery hear it, and they come forth at its call to the resurrection of a new existence.

There are periods in the experience of the freest nations, when the bravest will grow timid, and the most sanguine despond. They fancy, that civic worth has departed; they fear that degeneracy has set in. It is not, however, when men are anxious, but when they are indifferent, that times are really evil; it is not when many are complaining, but when all are careless, that degeneracy is present. There are seasons, when it would seem as if ten righteous men could not be found to save a city, yet, it is not that good men and true are wanting; they are only silent. Let the danger come, and not only ten, but ten thousand shall be upon the ramparts ; if the danger cries for more, more and yet more appear, to prove that the spirit of the fathers had not died, but only slept. Notwithstanding mistakes, prejudices, and perversions connected often with it, the patriotic sentiment is among the loftiest of our sentiments. A brave sentiment is that which so enthrones a disinterested conviction within his soul, that a man can act and suffer for the good of those whom he will never see. A brave sentiment is that which causes an abstract principle to be dearer to the heart, than the most enchanting fascinations with which the senses can tempt it. A brave sentiment is that which can enable a man to go to the dungeon as to a chamber of feasting, and to walk from the dungeon to a scaffold, as if it were a stage on which to receive acclamations to his triumph and his renown. Brave is that sentiment which makes light of life, compared with oppression or dependence ; yea, and not of life merely, but whatever clings most fondly about it, even home itself, ennobled with a wife's affections, and made bright with the smiles of childhood. Brave is that sentiment which renders a gory bed to the hero on the field where glory has been won, welcome as the bed of his bridal, and the blast of the trumpet which proclaims the victory, as pleasant to his soul, as the gladness of a nuptial song; brave is that sentiment which could so calm the spirit of a mountain peasant, and so steady his hand, as to hit with unerring aim the apple on his infant's head; a calmness of spirit and a steadiness of hand, imparted equally by love to his kindred, and hatred to their oppressors; fixed also by the strong resolve, that if the arrow which he shot, should reach the heart of his child, he had another in his sleeve which should reach the heart of his tyrant. A brave sentiment is that which despots have never been able to render odious; try to surround it as they might, with disgrace and infamy, it made the men who suffered for it, lovely even to those who trembled in the presence of their masters; those who dared not to openly imitate it, in silence did it homage; the victims met nothing but honor, at the last, and the tyrants nothing but execration.

And if the sentiment of patriotism evinces the greatness of its strength in sustaining those whose circumstances gave them fame, it still more evinces the greatness of its strength in sustaining those whose circumstances gave them nothing but oblivion; whose breath the dungeon drank, but whose existence has left no sign above its everlasting silence; whose death upon the scaffold was noted only to the bosoms which

it pierced ; whose bones lay unclaimed in the promis-
cuous carnage of the field ; or who, when all was over,
went back unheard of, to the quiet and the shadow of
industrious occupation, followed to their retirement by
no premium or no pæan. Nor less great is the sentiment in the high and honest souls, who, by their
usefulness and virtue, guard for their country the
good which they have received, and who improve for
their country the talents with which they have been en-
trusted. To the individual it matters not much, whether his name be widely sung, or whether it be little
known ; for the truth or falsehood of the spirit in which
he acts or suffers, must to him have its most important
result in his own solitary consciousness ; if there he
feels it to be a lie, the loudest vociferations of praise
are but noise and babble ; if he knows it to be a reality,
he has a joy which no obscurity can diminish, and no
calumny can overcloud.

In speaking of obligations implied in the spirit of
patriotism, it is easier to say, what they are not than
what they are. It is not one of these obligations to
think meanly of other countries. If this were a duty,
it would be a duty to be of most limited appreciation of
Providence and man ; it were a duty to resemble the
savage, both in his stolidity and his vanity. If it can
be no duty, but a vice, to cultivate such a state of mind

or feeling, no consideration can dignify or warrant the expression of it. If I cannot but feel that my country is the most desirable, and that I cannot but feel so upon the most dispassionate consideration, I have but little temptation to triumph over others, and having this faith, it is all the better that I should have it to myself. If I do not think so, there is no reason why I should say so; there is nothing, indeed, which ought to compel me to say so; and if refusing to belie my conscience and to do violence to my judgment, be treason, then let me be a traitor. I would try to look at my own country with calm discrimination, and others ought to expect that I should not look on theirs with any ungenerous prejudice; the evil that belongs to my own I would confess; the good that belongs to others I would not deny. In this I commit no offence against patriotism, but, if I did, the matter would not still be altered. Loyalty I do owe to my country; but I owe a higher loyalty to my own soul, to truth, to honesty, and to God. The things, however, do not clash or interfere; I do not dishonor my country by appreciating the excellence of another. I do it honor; for I show that it has reared in me a generous and a liberal man, and not a barbarian or a bigot.

Patriotism is not in all things to follow what the government of my country dictates, — nay, the noblest patriotism may call on me to denounce it, to denounce it boldly, and to oppose it bravely. If patriotism required more, patriotism would render me a slave, and that would be a contradiction, for a slave cannot be a patriot. Patriotism requires of me to obey the laws of my country, but patriotism equally requires of me to give my voice against such laws as I consider to be wrong; and if my ability is sufficient, it requires me to change them. In fact, patriotism requires me to study the good of my country, and no true citizen can ever suppose that moral iniquity can be national interest. A patriot " dares do all that may become a man; who dares do more, is none." And even if I should perceive that my country, in many points, compared unfavorably with others, that need not hinder me from loving it. No true, no natural attachment demands a blinded judgment or false encomium; and that attachment is the most lasting as well as the most elevated, which does not confuse the action of the intellect by the exaggerations of mere impulse. It is the noblest tribute which a man can offer; for in the cloudless sanity of his reason, he gives it with enlightened and unreserved devotion; he gives it with the truest promptings of his highest feelings, and he gives it with the full consent of his highest nature.

And, besides, comparisons are not only odious, but

in general they are ungraceful.   What can be more
ungraceful, than to glory in our wealth, power, dignity,
refinement ?   What, also, is often more absurd than
claims founded on superiority of national genius, when
what constitutes genius, has not been yet defined, and
when, if it were, it would be so hard to apply the
definition ?   Who is to say which evinces the greatest
intellectual capacity, — the practical mind of England,
the speculative mind of Germany, the artistical mind
of Italy, the theoretical mind of France, or the versatile
mind of this country ?   These, however, are harmless
comparisons ;   others are more irritating.   They are
such as lay claim to superior bravery, piety, and virtue.
Most nations worthy of any honor, are alike jealous of
these, and none can patiently bear to be especially
denied them.   They are right ; such qualities are the
life of character, and a country without character is
not a nation.   If it can submit to be thus stigmatized,
it is dead ; it is worse than dead, it breathes in contented infamy.   Nations will readily acknowledge that
they have not freedom ;   the want of wealth, they
regard as no disgrace ; but at insinuations against their
courage, their religion, or their morals, most justly they
are indignant.   The truth is, that we and all men,
judge nations other than our own, very partially in
these things, and often very falsely.   Physical courage,

I apprehend, is not very unequally distributed; and the influences which determine the relative positions of nations, must be traced much farther than to mere personal bravery. Many set down as no religion, or worse, that which is contrary to their own; but these are not the men to trust or to praise. God may be worshipped in places, where his worshippers do not pray as we do; the graces of heaven may descend as plenteously on their souls as on ours; and the dew of its blessing may be as refreshing on their lives.

Many judge the moral character of other countries than their own, it strikes me, with extreme injustice. They examine the statistics of crime; they sojourn for a time in leading cities; they roll along the highways; as they run they read, and as they read they write; they sum up the whole, they find that, from Dan to Beersheba, all is vicious; they return home, bless God that they have escaped out from lands of wickedness, and maintain, with an enthusiastic patriotism, that, in reaching their own, they have arrived in the only land of virtue. Here, again, there is need of modification. Our country is a part of our self-love; and, as we discern the vices of others more keenly than we do our own, so we do those which are not the vices of our country. Countries have their peculiar vices; they have also their peculiar virtues; but while the vices

may be seen of all men, the virtues are away from the
stranger's track.   We will not find a nation's virtues
standing upon its cross-roads ; we will not find a nation's
virtues strown over the surface of its cities.   To find
these in any country, we must pierce beyond the trod-
den path and the crowded street, to places where the
hearts are yet unworn and untravelled, and where, if
we see them with their besetting sins, we see them also
with their native graces.

After all, if, with the utmost candor, and the utmost
charity, we must believe other countries more vicious
than our own, it is a matter for sorrow, and not for
exultation.   I cannot think the spirit of a certain olden
prayer changed, because it is uttered in the plural rather
than in the singular ; I cannot think it more acceptable
to Heaven to say, " We thank God that we are not as
other men, or even as these publicans, than to say, I
thank God, that I am not as other men, or even as
this publican ; " for, judged by the catholic liberality
of the Gospel, the pharisaism of nationality is as odious
as any other kind of pharisaism.   Regarding then, as
we ought, moral evils in countries as in individuals,
with sorrow, and not with pride ; let us take this consolation along with us, that no nation ever stood, in
which the mass of excellence did not immeasurably
outweigh the mass of crime ; and that no society can

hold together without the bonds of integrity and goodness, without honesty and confidence in its dealings, without faith and purity in its households. The mere existence, then, of civilized communities, is evidence for worth ; for, where these exist in such communities, there are homes, and where there are homes, there must be virtue.

Anglo-Saxons stand conspicuous among the nations for their strength of patriotism ; but Anglo-Saxon patriotism, it must be confessed, has ever had more in it of the Roman than of the Christian spirit ; and the cases are not a few or trifling, in which it has evinced intolerance even more than Roman. The Anglo-Saxon is a manly race, yet is it more given to boasting than quite beseems its manliness ; the Anglo-Saxon is a great race, but somewhat less of self-sufficiency, and a little more of general amenity, would not ill become its greatness ; the Anglo-Saxon is a powerful race, but a power tempered by respect for others, would have rendered it more beneficent ; and instead of being, as it is, feared or hated through the world, it would have been trusted and loved. To say nothing of that passion for territory, and that lust of sway, which, since it first broke loose from German forests, have marked its course and signalized its history, it has borne hardly and harshly on every people who fell under its dominion ; and where it has not extinguished, it has enslaved them; it has given currency to many ideas of unscrupulous ambition, but to none more characteristic, than to that embodied in the maxim, " Our country, right or wrong." A saying more Anglo-Saxon, and yet more anti-Christian, was never uttered.

Let us look at the point involved. We have here no concern with disputes about the lawfulness of war. Assume at once, that it is right to defend, by force of arms, the honor, the claims, the independence, the existence of our country. Here we have covered, by our position, ground as extended as the most warlike patriot could desire; and even within these ample limits, the maxim has no application. For either our country is in the right, and we fight for the justice of her cause, or she is in danger of dishonor or destruction, and we fight for her salvation; we fight because we ought, or because we must; we fight from duty or necessity. In no case will men even suppose that they are fighting in the wrong. If it be answered, that the expression implies no more, than that the crisis of difficulty is not the time for inquiry, and that, when our country has need of our help, we should not wait to scrutinize when we should be prompt to act. Granted : we should give our country help, when danger calls for it, and we should give her all the help we can; but this civic duty cannot be aided by a doubtful maxim, which has either no meaning, or a meaning the most pernicious. For, will any man with a partial candor, assert that, independently of truth or justice, he may lawfully fight, if he fights only for his country? If, for instance, he only fight to enrich his country; if he only fight to enlarge his country; if he only fight, to gain for his country, not freedom, and safety, and independence, against tyranny and despotism, but a name to be a terror, a supremacy to be hated, a glory reeking in the fumes of carnage, and a history written in the blood of battles; no man will assert this; no man, whose moral being lives, will assert it; for such a doctrine would lay civilization in the dust; and the assertion, therefore, carries with it, its own refutation.

The maxim was not, I admit, intended for strict analysis or strict acceptation; but every such saying, by its brevity and point, obtains rapidly to popular currency; and if it involve a violation of eternal rectitude, is calculated to work interminably for mischief; the maxim, I acknowledge, was used but as a watchword for enthusiasm, in the hour of struggle. But, herein is its danger: a maxim like this, has all its danger from brilliant association, for it is such a one as deliberate reason, or sober common sense, or unclouded conscience, could have never suggested or adopted. If such a saying perished with the occasion, it would not much signify; but to confine it to that, either in its existence or application, is seldom possible; it may come from worthy struggle with the halo of success; it may come emblazoned with the glory of victory; it may come with loud rejoicings upon the trumpets of fame; it may come sad with the memory of departed heroes, or consecrated with the sanction of the surviving brave; it may pass from the sailor to the citizen, from the soldier to the civilian; from the commander to the magistrate; from the military camp to the legislative assembly; it may originate in the self-devotion of patriotism, but be appropriated by the artfulness of ambition, or by the cruelty of fanaticism. Then it admits of scarcely limit or corrective. There is no act, however wicked, if it can plead intention of benefit to the nation, which the maxim may not be used to justify; and there is no wickedness, however gigantic, which, according to this perversion, it has not comprehensiveness to grasp; it would acquit the tiger-monkey Robespierre, and it would canonize the ogre-demon Marat.

Patriotism, separated from justice and philanthropy, would not be a civilized virtue, but a savage vice ; patriotism, inconsistent with our large relations to humanity, would be a patriotism inconsistent with the Gospel. . If then, we cannot have the patriot, except on the ruin of the philanthropist and Christian ; give us the philanthropist and Christian, and we can spare the patriot. If we cannot have the hero without disobedience to God, and denial of Christ, let God and Christ be glorified as true, though every hero that has lived should be found a liar. Patriotism as a duty obliges no man to commit a wrong. On the contrary, the duty of patriotism is the most respected in the respect of every other duty ; and he is the greatest friend to his country, who is the greatest friend to virtue. It is thus that he can constantly befriend it, and ever give it his best support. " The times come but rarely, that try men's souls ; " but the times are always, when the virtuous citizen, in the humblest situation, is the best supporter of his country.

The virtuous citizen is a patriot, in the feeling of love that binds him to his country ; but, yet more seriously, in the obligations which he owes to his country. He is not often called on to pay these with his property or his blood ; but it is a debt which he pays not the less effectually, that he pays it peacefully and daily. He pays it by the industry with which he contributes, to prevailing comfort, and general prosperity. He pays it by whatever encouragement his talents, or his opportunities, enable him to give to works and undertakings of utility or embellishment. He pays it by adding his portion to the aggregate of nobleness and honor, that forms the national ideal, in which the heart of the patriot rejoices, which it is his glory to exalt, which he would have unstained as the cloudless sun, and of which he is more jealous than of life. He pays it by the encouragement of liberal arts ; by the encouragement of literature and science, not as things of mere utility alone, but as supplies also to higher wants, as means of uncorrupting pleasure, as attractions to draw men from grossness and selfishness, and as impulses to raise them in the scale of intelligent existence. He pays it by whatever he does to extend the sentiments of truth, good will and justice ; by whatever he does to make them clearer by his word or more impressive by his example. He pays it by any aid which he can give towards the formation of a wise and sound public opinion ; by any efforts that he applies to the rectification of popular errors ; by every sincere exertion to mitigate, if we cannot extinguish, the rancors of faction ; by every assuaging influence which he lets fall upon the strifes of passion. He pays it by any part which he takes in the agency that ameliorates laws, that removes the useless and the bad, and that strengthens the authority of the good. He pays it by reverence for law, and by obedience to it. He is not merely an enemy to his country, he is the enemy of civilization, he is the enemy of mankind, who sanctions outrage and anarchy in a community. He sets all order at defiance ; he spreads abroad alarm and dismay ; he tears down all civil rule, and tramples it in contempt ; and inasmuch as his actions are not simply a falling short of social harmony, but a direct resistance to it, he is worse than a savage.

The patriot-citizen pays his obligation to his country, by regarding, as among the most sacred of human pledges, any trust which his country commits to his keeping ; by feeling that he holds it for millions, present, and to come ; by feeling that, although he use it with the purest intention, his duty is neglected if he has not also labored to understand how it may be used to the most general advantage. Faithful to his trust, he is a noble spirit, whether it be small or large. To one it may be given to sustain the executive majesty of a nation ; to another, " the applause of listening senates to command ; " to another, to sit on the solemn tribunal of the magistrate, to hold the balance and to wield the sword of justice ; to another, nothing may be given except his elective suffrage, but in that he has the kingship of a freeman. Unnoticed, but with an honest heart, he casts it in, and is satisfied with the reward that comes in secret ; his heart is pure, and his hand is as clean as his heart ; there is no memory of a bribe, no consciousness of party passion, or of interested expectation, to sully the lustre of his spirit, or to disturb its calmness. Without distinction, or importance in the crowd, his mite goes into the treasury of his country ; and it is the mass which such unstained offerings form, that constitutes the genuine wealth which makes her truly rich, — the wealth of honor and of truth, without which there is not only no dignity, but no safety. The individual contributor may be lowly, but even for himself his offering is not lost. The eye which saw the widow in the throng near the temple of Jerusalem sees him too ; and as the simple grandeur of an upright soul conferred a value on her farthing beyond the gifts of princes, lofty integrity adds also a worth to his humble tribute, for which sword, sceptre, and ermine put together, would be no equivalents.

The patriotism which is worthy of this country, worthy of its advantages, worthy of its duties to the world, is a high and enlightened patriotism, a patriotism of loyal devotion, but also of enlarged philanthrophy. If man be only true, all here besides is full of inspiration and full of promise ; if man will be but faithful to his opportunities, all around him here is strong in noble energies. Every thing here tends to dilate the heart, to send it upward in gratitude to a fatherly God ; to send it outward in kindness to the brotherhood of man. The sky itself takes dimensions of grandeur, fitted to the glorious scope of empire which it overhangs. It is high, deep, broad, lofty, and should upraise the freeman's soul, whose step is on the freeman's earth. Nowhere is the calm more divinely fair ; nowhere is the storm more awfully sublime; nowhere does the sun shine forth with a more peerless majesty ; nowhere do the stars beam down with a more holy lustre. The atmosphere engenders no deadly plagues ; health lives in the breeze, and plenty comes teeming from the soil. Broad dominions, to be measured in leagues only by a scale of hundreds, snatch imagination from every belittling influence, and carry it out from narrow thoughts to an ennobling excursiveness. Then there are ocean lakes, in which kingdoms might be buried, and leave on the surface no ripple of their grave ; rivers, that sweep over half a world ; cataracts, eternal and resistless, that hymn forever the omnipotence which they resemble ; mountains, that stretch into the upper light, and mock, from their snow-crowned pinnacles, the clouds and the thunders that crash below them.

All these are your country's, but your country is
God's. It is God who has given you this country; it
is God who has enriched it with these grand objects,
and through these grand objects it is God who speaks.
He speaks in the chorus of your woods; in the tempests
of your valleys; in the ceaseless sobbings of your lakes
and oceans; in the vague, low murmurs of forest and
of prairie; in the mighty bass of water-falls, in the
silver melody of streams; and the voice that He sends
out from them is a voice for patriotism; but it is also a
voice for equity and a voice for goodness. Who can
look through the huge firmament; who can gaze upon
the golden fires with which it is studded; who can float
away on the wings of the spirit through the infinity of
stars; who can watch the roll of the torrent, pouring
out a sea in every gush, a sea of awful beauty; who
can thus put his soul into communion with the universe,
and not be enlarged by the communion? who can
really put his soul into communion with the universe,
and not be delivered from the slavery of prejudice
into the glorious liberty of humanity and of God?

The measure of your duty is the greatness of your
advantages, and the greatness of your advantages is the
standard to which you will be subjected in the judgment of Heaven and the judgment of history. You are
set for the hope or for the disappointment of the world.

With such a mighty country, with such inestimable privileges ; with such means of intelligence, virtue, and happiness ; with such means of increasing and dispensing them ; so young, and yet so strong ; so late, and yet so rich among the nations ; there is room to look for good interminably to future generations, which the one departing shall leave more abundant for the one that comes. In order that such anticipations be not empty dreams ; in order that they be not promises to change into mockery, vanity, and grief ; it should be the labor of a genuine and noble patriotism to raise the life of the nation to the level of its privileges ; to harmonize its general practice with its abstract principles ; to reduce to actual facts the ideals of its institutions ; to elevate instruction into knowledge ; to deepen knowledge into wisdom ; to render knowledge and wisdom complete in righteousness ; and to make the love of country perfect in the love of man.

ECONOMIES.

To begin, there is an economy of the individual. A true economy of the individual, implies a coördination of life with physical laws, not only because the body is the garment of an immortal soul, and should not be soiled or rudely torn; not only because it is the soul's earthly house, and should not be undermined; not merely because it is the soul's temple, consecrated by divine illumination, and should have no idols in its shrine, and no strange fire upon its altar; for it is more than all these to the soul, more than vesture to a wearer, than a dwelling to a tenant, than a temple to a worshipper; it is an inseparable element in that composite unity which now, in time, constitutes the living man. And to this whole living man, a life in coördination with these laws is that only which brings health and strength and power. Yet, not for mere health and strength and power; not even for their continuance, has coördination with these laws its most impressive value; not by length of days is this value to be measured. Length of days has no worth in itself. Length of days may be but a higher sort of vegetation; or it may be a long struggle with the stubborn wants of existence; or it may be a protracted succession of transmigrations from vanity to vanity; or it may be an enduring sentence to hard labor, self-pronounced and self-inflicted, from which death alone can give release, who will come at last to tell the convict that his term has expired, that he has collected gold enough, and may quit the prison. It is harmony with these laws that gives fitness for the highest labor, and susceptibility to the purest things. Without it, there can be no purpose in the will, no power in the act, no dignity in the being. Men become as walking shadows to the darkened eye and the disordered head; the heavens a pestilent collection of vapors, and earth a sterile promontory. The heart, made faint, trembles amidst scenes in which purer and braver hearts exult. The brain, enfeebled or bewildered, "in wandering mazes lost," dwells often in a region between the idiot and the madman, hovers, it may be, over him for a while, and then drops into the blackness of darkness forever. What to an untuned frame, in which remorse keeps company with discord, are the sweetness of prayer, the calls of duty, the electric tones of eloquence, the charms of art? To such a one, the whole of existence is unstrung, and all is hard, and not only unmusical, but also, hopeless. Daily society loses to him its vitality and its freshness, and opportunity after opportunity passes from the sphere of the possible to that of the impossible. Was it to one becoming thus insensate that the poet spoke?

> " O, how canst thou renounce the boundless store
>   Of charms which Nature to her votary yields, —
>   The warbling woodlands, the resounding shore,
>   The pomp of groves, the garniture of fields, —
>   All that the genial ray of morning yields,
>   All that answers to the song of even,
>   All that the mountain's sheltering bosom shields,
>   And all the dread magnificence of heaven, —
>   O, how canst thou renounce, and hope to be forgiven! "

A true economy of the individual, implies a coördination of the life with spiritual laws, with the law of thought, the law of conscience, and the law of goodness. How rich the life is, in which this is found; how poor, where it is not! Give a certain amount of capacity, and there is scarcely a limit to what may be accomplished by diligence, industry, and vital meditation. It is not knowledge alone that will be gained, but plastic command over it, — the heat that melts, and the talent that moulds it to the mind's command. The thing that appeared impossible, contemplated for a while, merely seems difficult, and after more intense regard the difficulty itself is gone; that which was dark and crude, as the mind broods upon it, emerges into light, and coming to the light, grows into order. And it may be, down below the whole there lies a lyric sweetness, to which, only, earnest and repeated struggles for articulation can afford a worthy utterance. Give the same amount of capacity, but with it connect indolence, listnessness, self-seeking, and self-indulgence, and years leave nothing but the ghosts of promises without performance, the remembrance of unsuccessful attempts, the conciousness of being beaten in the race, and despair of gaining the goal at any odds or in any way. When to this we add the vague ideas coming ever to the mind to mock it, telling it, like so many dim, but tormenting fiends, of all that it has lost; what treasures of memory, what stores of thought, what facility of execution, what abundance of fancy and emotion; all of which it might have had, but sought not rightly, — we have a case which it might seem hard to make more painful. Yet so it is not. Let the law of conscience be disregarded also, let the law. of goodness have been habitually violated, and then

the case is far more desperate. The moral faculties
give interest to all the others; they give them their
depth and significance. Untrue to these, we not only
waste the life, we kill it. It is not that the best affections languish, but they die. Even the faculties that
are purely intellectual suffer. To obtain the largest
possible result from our minds, we must be able to call
all their powers into action, into continuous action,
into concentrated action; and we must be able to do
this without compromise and without fear. Now, in
violating the moral laws of the spirit, we, in the first
place, corrupt the sources of culture, and circumscribe
its sphere, and lessen its means; we, in the second,
put the faculties themselves into hostility against it.
For how shall we dare to go to memory, if she can
open her book only to judge us; or to imagination, if
she has only demons with which to scare us; or to the
affections, if weepings and wounds are all that they
can show us? How shall we go to reason, even, if a
great portion of our ingenuity has been used in contrivances to blind or to deceive her, to silence her
voice, or to belie her counsel? And thus one part
of our spiritual existence must be smothered before
its birth, and another part must be stunted or strangled
in its growth. But connected with the moral laws, in
faithful and living union, there is no need of minute

detail to exhibit the wide range of being, and the glorious spheres of bliss and usefulness to which this capacity would attain.

No result can be obtained, if the laws of thought are disregarded. If they be fully and profoundly carried out, despite of disloyalty to conscience and to goodness, it is not to be denied that very imposing results may be had, of a certain kind. But imposing as they may be, do they subserve the true economy of an individual life? Connect thought with any of those strong passions which despise every law but their own, — is it, in its utmost success, the best order of an individual man? Suppose it aspires to become great, great by whatever distinction you please, but leaving out conscience and goodness, the inward heart of a man must be blank and poor, even when it has every thing else to fullness. Let a man have missed of no pleasure that he could enjoy, what of it all remains? Let a man have secured the most ample fortune, what has he in it, if he will pause but for one moment, and occupy that pause rightly, if conscience or goodness can have no place in it? The greatest soldier that ever lived is poorly engaged, if he be engaged only about his battles when his battles are over. The lives of such men are, for themselves, as little consistent with the best order of life, as those lives are which are wasted in the lower senses; while, for others, they are incalculably more injurious. What is the violence of a drunken clown to the ravages of a temperate Mahomet? "The ideal of morality," says Novalis, as quoted by Carlyle, "has no more dangerous rival than the ideal of highest strength, of most powerful life; which also has been named — very falsely, as it was here meant — the ideal of poetic greatness. It is the maximum of the savage. . . . . By this ideal, a man becomes a beast-spirit, a mixture; whose brutal wit has for weaklings a brutal power of attraction."

In the harmony of body, spirit, and estate would consist the completeness of the individual. Economy of the individual includes not the man alone, but his adjuncts also. Economy, as merely applied to thrift and foresight, has a solemn meaning; and the possession of it, or the want of it, has most important bearings on individual power and individual destiny. Qualities are these which, even as thus practically understood, often spring from the best faculties of our nature, and enable us to exercise these best faculties in their divinest spheres. "It is better to give than to receive;" and it is economy, in its humblest meaning, yet its highest, which enables many a lowly soul to translate this precept into practice. Many a story of god-like beauty might be written under this title, and many a tragedy. The tragedy would not be confined to the griefs which want of economy has brought home to individual hearts, but would include wide-spread woes, which it has brought on cycles of generations and realms of nations. The same tragedy is still omnipresent, — in hearts, in homes, in states, in sorrows, in suicides, in struggles, — working with the sadness that cannot speak, with the misery that despairs, with the convulsions that only a benignant Power above us can assuage.

The harmony, we have said, of body, spirit, and estate, forms the completeness of the individual man. The derangement of this harmony, by the sacrifice of the spirit to the body, can never be otherwise than guilty and degrading. It is not so with regard to the sacrifice of the body to the spirit. Sometimes, it is true, this may be fanaticism; sometimes it may be folly; but never is it gross. It may be the highest right, and the highest right it is, to consign the body to hunger, to nakedness, to peril, to torture, to prison, and to death, when the higher life demands the lower. And this, we suppose, is the meaning of that great saying which declares, that, when a man " loses his life " in obedience to a holy faith, he " gains " it. Sacrifices thus made, are truly grand. Sublime was that immolation which Milton made to the honor of

his country, when he laid his sight upon the altar of
its defence ; and yet more sublime was that offering
of life which the immortal Howard made to the good
of his race, of a life which he spent in the depths of
European prisons, which he lost in an Asiatic wilderness. Neither can we help admiring the intellectual
enthusiasm which, even without result, may consume
the body before its time. Though the body perish,
we cannot mourn, while the soul can live, should it
live but in one choice memory ; but when it lives in
memories without number, then we have reason only
to rejoice. It is not permitted us to lament, while the
soul abides in the thinker or the writer, whose visible
presence, indeed, disappears, but whose being continues in immortal words or in immortal facts. And
that rapture, that rapture unto death, which flashes
glory on the painter's canvas, which cries with wildness in the poet's song, wretched would it be for cold
prudence to condemn, rejoicing as we do in its light,
and charmed as we are by its sound. When the spell
has left us, sorrow, and not judgment, comes back
with the thought, that the hand is stiff which illumined
the canvas, that the heart is quenched which fired the
the song.

Much less genius is lost to the world than the world
fancies ; still, there is genius lost. Every generous

man who has risen to fame, has some one to speak of, as one who deserved fame, but missed it. He will tell us of his rare intellect, of his deep philosophy, of his soul-filled eloquence, and all this he will say of his friend with an impassioned faith in what he might have been, and what he could have done. If this friend has left among men any fragments of his power, he traces out for us the design, of which these fragments were but parts; and haply he completes the plan. Yet, ever comes lament along with admiration, and ever, as he praises, he will confess that somewhat was wanted to carry promise to fulfilment. Incompleteness, in any form, is distressing. Structures in ruin sadden the heart, structures unfinished chill it. The walls which had once a roof, that gave living men a shelter, are not so desolate as those which never were covered; and the hearth whereon fire has burned, is not so lonely as that which bears no mark at all of flame or of smoke. The aisles and cloisters that have ere now, however, long ago, been quickened by meditation and by prayer, wake up the soul, yet calm it; the temple nobly planned, advanced half way, then abandoned, excites nothing but disturbing thought. Incompleteness in the humblest life is painful; how affecting, then, in any life which opened with the prophecy of being a great one! But is not a complete life, a thing as yet to be looked for, whatever the kind or the degree of power? The world has had many a great man; but that man who would peacefully and proportionately fill, in all its roundness, the circle of his being, must be formed in some age different from ours; and to the utmost faith in progress, such a one must long be the "coming man."

No finite individuality is absolute. The individual human being exists no more separately than the individual atom. The laws which govern his nature bind him to others, and others to him, with enlarged and multiplied relations. There are, therefore, economies wider than that of the individual; and next beyond, we say, there is the economy of home.

Home is a genuine Saxon word; a word kindred to Saxon speech, but with an import common to the race of man. Perhaps there is no other word in language that clusters within it so many and so stirring meanings, that calls into play, and powerfully excites, so many feelings, so many faculties of our being. "Home,"—say but the word, and the child that was your merry guest begins to weep. "Home,"—play but its tunes, and the bearded soldier, that blenched not in the breach, droops, and sickens, and dies. "Home,"—murmur but its name, and memories start around it that put fire into the brain, and affections that almost suffocate or break the heart, and pictures that bewilder fancy with scenes in which joy and sorrow wrestle with delirious strife for possession of the spirit. " Home," — what does it not stand for, of strongest, of most moving associations ! — for childhood's grief and gladness, — for youth's sports, and hopes, and sufferings, and passions, and sins, — for all that brightened or dimmed the eyes, — for all that convulsed or tranquillized the breast; for a father's embrace, or for his death-bed, — for a mother's kiss, or for her grave, — for a sister's love, or a brother's friendship, — for hours wasted, or hours blest, — for peace in the light of life, or fears in the shadows of perdition. Home, when it is all that nature and grace can make it, has a blessedness and beauty of reality that imagination, in its fairest pictures, would find nothing to excel. But in many a spot called home, neither nature nor grace is found. A collection of home histories, honestly set down, would be a rich contribution to materials for the philosophy of character. Not gay, not pleasant, not innocent, would all of these home histories be. Not a few of them would be sad, dreary, wretched, and within the earliest dwelling of man would be discovered the appropriate opening of many a tragic life.

And yet nothing can humanity worse spare than pleasing and gracious memories of home. So fervently does humanity cling to what nature owes it, that those who have no home will make one for themselves in vision. Those who have an evil one will soften down its many vices, and out of the scantiest affections bring forth rays of the heart to brighten their retrospect. It is the miracle of the five loaves performed spiritually for the soul, lest the instincts of our humanity should faint and perish by the way. The visitings of early home thoughts are the last to quit us. Feeble age has them, when it has nothing else in memory; and when all the furniture which imagination put together has gone to pieces and to dust, these, not constructed, but planted, planted down in the living soil of primal consciousness, flourish to the last; when the treasures which experience has been many years collecting a few months may seem to take away, some diamonds are left behind, which even the thief, Time, has spared reminiscences that glimmer through bare and blank obscurity from the crevices of youth. As every thing human has an element of good in it, that which is good in a vicious home is what the past gives back to feeling; it is also that which is good in an evil man that the remembrance of a virtuous home acts on.

There is no mist of guilt so thick that it can always exclude the light of such remembrance; no tempest of passion so furious as always to silence its voices. Dur-

ing a lull in the hurricane of revelry, the peal of the
Sabbath bell may come along the track of wasted years,
and, though loaded heavily, will be not unkindly in its
tones. Through the reekings of luxury, faces that
beamed on the prodigal in youth may seem to start in
trouble from the tomb, and, though marred with grief,
though pallid with affliction, turn mildly towards him,
not in anger, but in sorrow. Amidst the chorus of
bacchanals and the refrains of lewdness, the satiated
libertine may fancy, at moments, that he hears the calls
of loved ones gone to heaven, startling him from the
trance of death. Under the loud carousals that rage
above the brain, deep down and lonely in his heart,
there may come to him the whisper of parental exhortation, the murmur of household prayer, and the music
of domestic hymns. The very criminal in his cell will
often have these visitations ; ministers to exhort, not
enemies to accuse ; angels to beseech, not demons to
scoff. The sentenced culprit, during even his last night
on earth, must sleep, and perchance may dream, and
seldom will that dream be all in the present and in
prison ; not all of it, if any, will be of chains and blood,
of shapeless terrors and pale-faced avengers, of the
scaffold and the shroud. Far other things will be in
the dream. He once was honest, and spent his childhood, it may be, in a rustic home, and grew to youth

amidst laborious men and with simple nature. Out of imagery thus derived will his dream be formed. In such dreams will be the green field and the wooded lane ; the boat sleeping on the stream ; the rock mirrored in the lake ; the shadow, watched expectingly from the school-room window, as it shortens to the noontide hour. Then there will be parents, blessed in their unbroken circle ; there will be young companions, laughing in their play ; there will be bright harvest evenings, after days of healthful toil ; there will be family greetings, thanksgiving feasts ; there will be the grasp of friendship, there will be the kiss of love. The dream will not be entirely, if at all, a dream of crime, disgrace, and death ; it will be one that reproduces, on the brink of eternity, the freshness of emotion, hope, and desire with which existence on earth began. What is put into the first of life is put into the whole of life. This should never be forgotten.

The true economy of the home is not mechanical, but moral. The household is not a machine, not a collection of pulleys and springs, which it needs but skill in directing force to manage. The household is an assemblage of kindred spiritualities, a system of gradations ; an association, in various stages of human intelligences and human wills ; and these can as little be harmonized by the command of authority as by the use of power. To control, and yet not enslave, — to leave free, and yet not abandon, — is a great problem in government, whether its sphere be a household or an empire. In the household, control and freedom can be reconciled only by wisdom and the affections. Love is the mediator between power and dependence; that which meekens authority, that which ennobles submission. Love is the holy and living bond, both of the equal and the unequal; that which changes the rigor of mutual claims into the grace of mutual kindness; that which brings courtesy into agreement with sincerity, and harmonizes deference with independence. Only love can subdue the selfish will in either doing or forbearing; only this can give sweetness to command, cheerfulness to obedience, and unity to companionship.

Wider still than the economy of home, there is an economy of the State.

The state, as well as the family, is an organic unity and a social necessity. It is no more a thing of chance or a thing of choice, that men dwell together in nations, than that they dwell together in families. The idea of the state is, therefore, as permanent as that of the household. The origin of neither can be found in the dictates of prudence or the principles of calculation. They exist irrespectively of the pleasurable or painful experience of the individuals who compose them. The individual may be wretched as the member of a family, he may be miserable as the member of a state, and the influences which make him so may be found within the family and within the state. The order of humanity, however, necessitates both the family and the state, though it does not necessitate the wretchedness and misery. But man is not a member of the state in the same way in which he is a member of the family; not by the same class of instincts, not by the same class of sentiments. To rule the state, therefore, by the methods of the family, would be quite as mischievous as to rule the family by the methods of the state.

Though the state, when most excellent in its actual form, cannot but be imperfect, its worst constitution is better than barbarism or anarchy. But the idea of it rises above all forms, dimly glimmers through the basest, clearly shines through the noblest, and, whether in the one or the other, stands for grand conceptions of the social nature; for order, for security, for freedom, justice, activity, and culture. Scarcely ever has any tyrant been so brutal, as not, in some pretence of zeal for these, to find excuse for shedding the blood of his victims. There is much that is impressive, almost sacred, in this idea; not to the superstitious alone, but to the most sober; not by tradition only, but by its intrinsic essence. Who does not feel the truth of our position, when in the presence of any human being in whom the majesty of a nation is impersonated? It is not merely the man that awes him, or the office, but the idea, — the idea in his own soul, which transcends the man, which transcends the office. Parliament or congress, statute, decree, or ukase, has from this its living life, and without it they were but as blotted paper, or as the leaf that shivers idly in the wind. King, president, or kaiser has from this his greatness; and though sceptres be broken, and thrones be fuel for garret fires, though monarchs drop one after another into beggars' graves, still the idea remains; nay, as time advances and virtue grows, it will spread more and more of its luminous beauty over the world.

Loyalty, then, is something more than devotion to a person, it is more than reverence for an office; it is an appreciation of the idea, of which the person is only the minister, and the office a type. Patriotism is something more than zeal for the material interests of our country; it is zeal for its elevation in all that elevates man. This cannot fail of admiration, whether it support certain modes of government, or oppose them. History celebrates with equal glory numbers of great souls, of whom some did the one, and some did the other. The monarch Alfred was a patriot as well as the republican Washington; and the patriotism of Hampden or Sir Harry Vane is as little to be doubted as that of Leonidas or Socrates. All these lived or died in true devotion to their supreme idea; and many, we may hope, as noble there have been, whom no history has been found to celebrate. A Grecian mariner once entered the temple of Neptune, to place his portrait in it as a votive offering, expressive of gratitude for his escape from shipwreck. The priest, pointing to the many pictures given by individuals in circumstances like his own, urged the fact as a rebuke to neglect, and as an argument against skepticism. "But where," inquired the sailor, "are the pictures of those who were drowned?" So, when we walk through the majestic temple of the past, and the Genius of history, as the priest of that temple, points to the portraits of the godly and the great which every age has contributed, may not we, too, ask, "Where are the pictures of those who were drowned? Where are the pictures of thousands who, in their day, did not only vow, but strive, who yet were swallowed in the stormy surges that roll above eternal and deep oblivion?"

Whatever be the form of government, the state in its true purpose is for all. Every violation of this principle is an evil; and the measure of the evil is the degree of the violation. The state is not for the magistrate, but the magistrate for the state; and magistrate and state are, both of them, for man. The character of a genuine freedom is, to give every individual a living position in the state; and the essence of a sound civic morality is, to cause the individual to feel that he does not act for himself or for a part, but for the whole. In this sense, he who wields the sceptre is not more for all than he who plies the shuttle. Where, indeed, the mechanism of government is well constructed, less depends on the individual than where it is not, and certain coarse results cannot fail to be obtained. Yet if no positive evils were consequent on dearth of thought and dearth of principle, if no force of selfishness and no prevalence of corruption could injure or impede the working of the machine, still all the finer, grander, purer influences of the state upon society are lost. Politics are, therefore, social morals in their widest range; not, indeed, politics as meant in the party battles of the hour, but as the application of immutable principles to civic conduct.

The best condition of the state is that which stimulates individual energy, and yet combines all social forces into tranquil harmony. That is the best condition of the state, in which the state so regulates its own activities, as to prevent convulsion in itself and confusion in its members; which, having organic stability, yet capacity for expansion, has security for order and vitality for progress. That is the best condition of the state, in which the man is never lost in the institutions, but in which the institutions, by inward and by outward culture, tend to strengthen and build up the man. The power of the state is wisely and well used, when it fosters, not the works alone that enrich the person, but those also which enrich the public. The wealth of the state, or the wealth of the person, is wisely used, and well, in giving grandeur to these works, in adding ornament to utility, in shedding splendor on the profitable, and in rendering every structure connected with national activity a monument of national magnificence. Art, even for its own sake, is not extravagance, but surest thrift. Add literature to art, and the saving is increased. Art and literature adorn the memory of a people when their dominion is no more. The fragments of the beautiful, that lie scattered over a nation's grave, win from eras that follow affection and admiration. After-times rake the ashes for these broken relics, and they strive to imitate when they can neither rival nor restore.

Deeper, broader than all states, there is an economy of the universe; and this is an economy that includes and embraces an economy of our race.

Not mere bulk of bodies, not mere vastness of space,

constitutes this economy of the universe; but power, power boundless, ceaseless, intelligent, whose agencies we term laws, for want of language more exact. Laws, thus regarded, stand for supreme action and supreme intellect, as we apprehend them in the universe. Answering to forms in our own spirits, they reveal to us that we live in the midst of thought and care. We recognize the law of order, or power directed by pure intellect. The results of power, as thus discerned, are simply dimensional and dynamical, results true to the utmost rigor of geometry and mechanics. Strip the earth of its foliage, reduce it to a naked sphere; shear the sun of his beams, sweep the stars of their light; yet these blank orbs, desolate and dead, would contain all the data that abstract science requires. Mysterious, however, does this nature of ours appear, when we reflect that this science, which unites the mind with the universe, determines the order and character of remotest facts by conditions of a present reason, and that the phenomena which realize the thought, are independent of the thinker. He cannot say, " Let them be; " but he does say, " They are," and " Thus they are," — " They will be," and " In such or such a manner will they be." So, accordingly, they are, or so they are to be. The assertion and the prophecy are absolute. A man dogmatically propounds that the constitution of our system requires another planet. He bases his position upon pure calculation. "This planet," he says, "must be;" and this planet is.

Discernible in the universe, likewise, is the law of wisdom, or power directed by the practical intellect. The connection and continuity of means and ends, infinitely extended, and everlastingly sustained, is in harmony with human thought, in fact, is a necessity of human being. Experience, which is the life of the practical intellect, within the limits of man's faculties, depends on this connection and continuity. In the same manner we discern supreme wisdom through the universe in the multitude and suitableness of its provisions, and particularly in relation to ourselves. Every thing within discovered regions has its use; every such thing is sufficient for its use. Nothing is below this, and nothing beyond it. There is as much light as we can bear; as much motion, too; and so much as we require of each, so much we have. From the tint of a flower to the lustre of a star, from the structure of a pebble to the orbit of a comet, all are balanced and adjusted, all answer the conditions of their existence. While thus the quantities of things accord exactly in measure to the want of them, and their qualities are in strict relation of fitness to supply it, there is at the same time a plenitude, an abundance, that is endless and exhaustless. Energy, omnipotent energy, is audible every where in music, is visible every where in beauty; and the very arrangement that reveals its grandeur, puts a veil upon its terrors.

Especially does the universe manifest the law of goodness, or power directed by the loving intellect. This, indeed it is, that gives God reality to the soul, and, void of it, all nature would be but an infinite and dismal sepulchre. Discern, through existence, divine love as the perfect spirit acting on your consciousness, all agencies in creation, and all excellence in man, become then as ministers of God; life in the motion of a worm; happiness in the song of a bird; beauty in the flash of a gem, as in the glow of noon; charity in the widow's mite, as in an angel's gift; religion sublime in the rustic's prayer, not less than in the martyr's hymn. Life has no number for its gradations, for its extent there is no measure; and according to the order and compass of every animated being, the prevailing condition of life is happiness. According to the scale of nature, God gives it to the fly whose buzz is on the sunny air, as he does to the loftiest soul that rejoices in the light of thought, and glories in the strength of action. Beauty in the universe, is yet as wide as life, and beauty is all for man. Beauty, indeed, is divine life, in form, in hue, in sound, in consciousness ; spread over the earth, spread over the sea, filling the great dome of heaven ; painted on the brain, panting in the heart ; kingly in the might of man, celestial in the purity of woman ; every where, in all things, sacred and undying ; the language and the sign of the fit and fair, the utterance that breathes, and the glow that blooms from the eternal Mind.

Does not this supreme economy enter directly into the concerns of our species ? Surely it does, in a universal and constant Providence. Here it works, mostly, through the ministry of man ; and every man, be he conscious of it or not, is its agent, and fulfils some purpose for it, whether he hold a plough or found an empire, whether he be a malefactor or a martyr. That which is stupendous in the visible world, has grown by means that are unseen. The spring that feeds the stream, and the stream that feeds the river, are remote and unnoticed in silence and in shadow. Similarly placed, are the sources and tributaries which swell those currents that rush through courses of mighty destinies, and gather to the forces of stupendous power. The sword, terrible instrument as it is, of human passion, is made to work for good. Even by this, the wrath of man is compelled to serve the purposes of God. But, happily, the lyre is more effective than the sword, and more enduring. The living thought in the living word, and the living word in music; this it was that first charmed men out of barbarism; nor has it lost its power yet, and its power cannot yet be spared. Much of humanity's education has been lyrical. History, at one time, was song; so were laws; so was worship; so was prophecy; so was philosophy; and though annals, decrees, prayers, predictions, wisdom, have become independent of verse or chant, yet that which was truth in them, comes down even to our own time, and still mingles in the everlasting harmony of life.

To assume that we understand the plan of Providence, were daring presumption; but to rest in a plan is a necessity of reason, a necessity of faith. The origin, growth, decay, and death of nations coexist with the life, the integrity, and the progress of our race. This is no fortuity. Certainty and simplicity of result come out from the caprices and contrarieties of human freedom. This is no fortuity. The army of our species is, indeed, endless, and we who speculate on its destination, are closed up in a division of its ranks. We cannot quit our place to take a stand out of this army and above it, to see whence it has come and whither it is going. Yet, onward as we march, we catch views of Calvary and of other elevations along the path of time; and from these we can take note that we are under guidance, and not without a goal.

Thus wonderful and numberless are the relations of our being. In alluding to past ages, it is common to speak of them as dead, to speak as if we were standing on a grave. This is not true of humanity in the aspects in which we have been contemplating it. The ages are all vital, and over life, and not on death we tread. Humanity is as an inverted pyramid, and every stratum of it, from the point below to its upward surface, is bound each to each by links of living mind. Over this wide surface, and down into the darkest depths, man understands man, wherever he travels or explores. The philosopher, rich in all the lore of wisdom, is yet a brother, and can feel his fraternal relation to the savage of Australia. The man of this century is not cut off from the man whose existence can be traced in the profoundest abyss of time. Bring up from that abyss the darkest hieroglyphic, the man of this day pierces into its meaning and finds out its interpretation; bring up the smallest remnant of moulded clay, bring up the most rugged fragment of sculptured brass, at once he says, — "The image and superscription are here of a spirit like my own; and though forty centuries lie between us, we are united by our souls." More properly, perhaps, should we find the diversity of our nature, in capacity and condition, symbolized by the creature in the first vision of Ezekiel. With feet to pace the earth, with wings to mount to heaven, with hands beneath the wings to work, fourfold in face, was this creature; and so is humanity. Backward it looks, and forward also, to the actual and the possible. Each face, too, was different, and each we may take to indicate some elevated mental or moral quality : the face of a man, conscience and intelligence; that of a lion, courage; that of an ox, patience; that of an eagle, aspiration. The creature of the prophet's trance was in the centre of wheel within wheel, glistening all around with eyes. So it is with humanity : it is in the centre of circle within circle of eternity and mystery; and though the compass of its own light be only as a speck, it is embosomed in the watchfulness that comprehends immensity and that never sleeps.

The individual, then, is not mechanically, but vitally, related to the whole empire of existence. The farthest star that a man can see is a part of his life; nor is this life of his severed from stars that never will be seen. Day and darkness, the seasons, the elements, vegetation, animal beings, are not mere adjuncts of his existence; they are portions of it. The sentiment of kindred binds the individual man to his family ; the social sentiment binds him to the community ; the patriotic, to his country ; the human, to his race. The moral sentiment binds him to men by duty, and the religious binds him to God by faith. The life of a man is not, like that of a brute, in his blood, but in his spirit, and all is the life of a man that he can embrace within the consciousness of his spirit. If a man's spirit had the range of the outward creation by sense, if human history were its memory, if its reason comprehended all known and possible truth, if its imagination were adorned with all that is lovely, if its character had all goodness, this, then, would be the range of its life. Though far from such perfection, yet the actual life of the most bounded consciousness spreads in its relations into unbounded being.

Is the time ever to come, when humanity shall be in full completeness and harmony ? Is the time ever to come, when humanity in the individual shall be strong and independent, — in the family, wise and gracious, — in the state, just and disinterested, — in the church, believing, charitable, tolerant, — when the savage shall be raised, when the heathen shall be converted, when the grossest shall be civilized, and the worst restored, — when every man, being true to his position, shall be one with his race, and his race, being accordant with its origin and its end, shall be one with God ? This may always be but an idea; yet, even as an idea, it has deep and living power. It is a sublime thought. Wherever it is strong, it kills the narrow self, and is at the bottom of all continued and admirable action. " Worlds," says Fichte, " speaking out of this faith in the infinite, produce worlds. Ages produce ages, which stand in meditation over those that have gone before, and reveal the secret bond of connection which unites causes and consequences within them. Then the grave opens, — not that which men heap together in earth, but the grave of impenetrable darkness, wherewith the first life has surrounded us, and from out of it arises the mighty power of ideas, which sees in a new light the end in the beginning, the perfect in the partial ; every wonderful work which springs from faith in the Eternal appears, and the hidden aspirations which are here imprisoned and bound down to earth soar upward on unfettered pinions into a new and purer ether."

As the individual is vitally related to the universe, so is the universe to the individual. All the powers of nature contribute to his wants. They are ministers to the requirements of his body, and to the faculties of his soul. The earth gives him of her fullness ; the winds are his servants ; the mines are his treasure-places ; the mountains are his watch-towers ; the clouds refresh him with shade and showers; the sun covers him with splendor; above his head are the heights of air, and beneath his eye the depths of ocean. All energies are working to support, to educate, to bless him; and not these only, but whatever men have done or suffered, whatever has made the life of ages, .whatever has made the life of nations. The whole has been acting for the individual soul. For that, patriarchs had visions sent them from the opened heavens. For that, prophets beheld a glory to be revealed in distant times. For that, Jesus himself appeared in the world, was wounded with many griefs, and bled upon the cruel cross. For that, Evangelists have written and Apostles preached. For that, philanthropists have worked and lived. For that, martyrs have endured and died. For that, philosophers have meditated, and poets have sung, and wisdom and melody have been born. For that, earth is robed in fairness, and heaven is hung with lamps of gladness. For that, all governments, all dynasties, all hierarchies, have existed; and that shall be when they shall be no more. When monarchy, with its gorgeous pomp and haughty sway, its solemn power and its towered palaces, shall have melted as a dream, — when democracy, with its din of tongues and turbulence, shall be silent as an infant's sleep, — nay, when this huge globe itself shall shake to atoms all that rest upon its surface, as a lion arousing from slumber throws from his mane the dews of the forest, — when the sun shall be dark, and even the mighty hosts of stars shall die, — that soul, that sacred soul, shall live. That spirit, kindled in the breath of Deity, has a light to burn over the ashes and the graves of worlds, — a light of joy and thought for ever, in the consciousness of its immortal being, in the consciousness of its eternal Lord.

Yet glory not, thou proud man! for, in the midst of these sublime realities, thy pride belittles thee. Thou hast not the faith to which things invisible are open; thou hast not the humility to which greatness is revealed. And, thou timid and desponding man, cheer up thy hope, and let thy confidence not fail thee. Think not the distant stars are cold; say not the forces of the universe are against thee; believe not that the course of things below is a relentless fate; for thou canst see the stars, thou canst use the forces; in right, thy will is unconquerable, and by it thou art the maker and the lord of destiny. In thy living consciousness the universe itself has living being, and thou in that art greater than the universe. Anoint thine eyes with holy thought, that the gross and fleshly scales may fall from off them. Then, like Gehazi in the mountain at the prayer of Elijah, thou shalt behold that Power for thy good is round about thee; thou shalt discern that thou art embosomed in Protection, — that thou art compassed by the fiery energies of Heaven, — that thou art girded and guarded by the Presence and the Majesty of God.

MUSIC.

I WANT to express to you some vague notions that lie crudely in my mind, on the subject of music. You need fear no technicalties; for of music, as a science, I know nothing. I merely intend to consider it in relation to our general humanity, and in relation to those impressions which it is its object to make on universal sensibility. Writing freely, as I do, I am not ambitious of unity or of order; and therefore, whatever feelings or incidents, suggested by the present topic, come to my mind, shall also come to my pen.

Memory is the faculty with which music has the most endeared and the most inspiring connection; for memory it is that revives experience, and experience it is feeds emotion. We soon begin to live in memory, either by discovery or delusion. What we have been is soon more pleasant to us than what we are likely to

be ; and ever and anon our ,truant thoughts retrace
their ways, and feel the hours too short, that once had
seemed too long. The slightest and most unexpected
analogies call before us the scenes of other days ; the
finest thread of association has a strength to pull us
back to the Eden or the wilderness of departed hours.
The odor of a flower will make the field bloom with
ethereal softness to our fancy, and in fancy we have
in them again our childhood's gambols ; the whistle of
a bird will give us to the sunny groves, where we read
and mused, where we slept and dreamed ; a river, like
one that flowed near the dwelling of our youth, in which
we angled and in which we bathed, will annihilate half
a century ; it is the same bright sun that gilds its surface ; it is the same clear sky that beams from its
cloudless waters ; and we are not awakened to reality
until we catch the shadow of a wrinkled face mocking
at our fantasy. A countenance, passed rapidly in the
street, by the force of affectionate remembrance, will
cause us to forget that one we loved has long been
formless in the dust. And so, the vapors of a summer's morning, hanging sleepily on meadow or on
mountain, or the chase of brilliant clouds in the gorgeous heaven of an autumn evening, will reanimate
the past within us, in musings that we cannot shape,
and in recollections that we cannot define. I was

about to compare their influence to that of music, but I am going to speak of music itself.

The music which touches our primitive emotions, we feel at once; complicated and high-wrought harmony we must hear often before we can appreciate. But harmony is not, on this account, the less exalted or the less excellent. A song which sweetly expressed a single sentiment would delight a thousand, and ten of the thousand would but faintly appreciate the choral verse of Dryden's "Alexander's Feast." A pathetic ballad can move a multitude, but few in this multitude would read the "Paradise Lost," and fewer still would enjoy it. And so in music; compared with those whom a pleasing melody can charm, the number is small whom the might of Handel, or the magic of Bethoven, can profoundly ingratiate; while those who have no sympathy with loftier music depreciate what they do not comprehend, as many also affect an admiration which they do not feel. From indiscreet enthusiasts, or from ignorant pretenders, a cant has begun to prevail in musical criticism, which, if not the most tormenting of all cants of criticism, is the most unintelligible. Men, who thus rave, will talk to you as if musical sounds had the definite significance which arbitrary usage gives to words. But it is not so; and, in the nature of things, cannot be.

The direct relation of music is not to ideas, but emotions; suggestive, certainly it is, but suggestive to each mind, with an indefinite variety of association. Test this position.   Take, for example, any given combination of sounds, and let the effect be startling and sublime; ask, then, two men, whose imaginations have been trained in different modes of life, each to offer an interpretation; each will explain it in his own way, and each, though contrary to the other, may not be inconsistent with the original.   Suppose these two men to be a sailor and a soldier.   The sailor will call it a thunder-storm, and the soldier will maintain it as a battle.   By what peculiarity of sound can the specific difference be determined?   By what rapid shrillness may a flash of lightning be implied, which will not, with as correct analogy, imply a flash of powder? and what heavy movements of deep bass will call to mind the rolling of thunder, that may not as naturally represent the rolling of cannon?   If any zealot for the precision of musical expression should tell me, that military airs could easily be so interspersed as to distinguish a battle from a tempest, I say it is little to the purpose, if the sounds which should directly suggest the conflict, do not, without mistake, suggest it.   To criticise music, as if it had the qualities which belong to articulate speech, is to put it in positions as ludicrous as some characters were wont to hold in the ancient drama, in which one man represented a wall, and another a grove, and in which each was obliged to indicate his part by saying, "I am the wall," "I am the grove." Every art has its own limit; and to endeavor to convey it beyond that, tends to degrade it from genius to quackery.

From the very fact that music is not bound to a rigid and arbitrary articulation, it is the most spiritual, the most impressive, and the most universal of all arts; it is, thence, the voice of humanity, for it is the voice of the heart. Poetry and music act on the same elements of our nature, but in a diverse method. Poetry awakens emotion by means of thought, but music awakens thought by means of emotion. The effect of music is more immediate and intense than that of poetry, but the impression of poetry is more indwelling and more lasting. Poetry, also, has the great advantage, that its power can be carried to the heart at once, and does not need, as music, an agency, which, even in moderate skill, cannot always be commanded, and that in perfect skill can rarely be found. Music, however, in the works of its greatest masters, is to me more marvellous and more mysterious than poetry; of all that proceeds from creative genius, I regard it as the most wonderful emanation. The spirit of a sublime poet, however remote from me, is not beyond my conception; but that of a sublime musician, is enshrouded from my ken within a sanctuary which my imagination has never been able to pierce.

Listen, for instance, to a complete orchestra, in the performance of any noble musical composition, be it opera or oratorio, mass or symphony, and you will apprehend what I am unable to explain. Now a strain, almost rudely simple, comes upon your ear, then there rolls a swell of harmony hugely onward, as the waves of ocean; now there are tones of sorrow, then a burst of choral gladness; now groanings from the depths of a wounded spirit, then gushings of praise, such as angels might have shouted when earth was born into sunshine; now, the wrangling discords of anger, then, the wild incoherencies of madness; then, the breathings of holy thoughts, the purity of saintly feelings, so chastened that they seem not for the coarse air of our hard world, so celestial that they seem fit only for the harps of seraphs. What imaginations must they have been, in which all these were conceived aforethought! what a combination of reckless enthusiasm with consummate art! what a union of the spontaneous and the reflective, of the instinctive and the æsthetical!

Marvellous as the variety is in all the most glorious

music, the unity of it is yet more marvellous ; unity of spirit, unity of purpose, and unity of effect. Consider the mechanism by which this unity is to be produced, the arrangements and adjustments of so many sounds, with so many modes of producing and combining them, in song, hymn, anthem, symphony — in all harmonies of dramatic fancy, sacred and secular ; these things, then, considered, tell me whether an inventive and a creative musical genius is not, in the known works of God, among the rarest and the most surprising.

The desire for popular effect has injured music, as in these days it has injured every other art. And the mischief, as in the case of all permanent mischief, has come from the abuse of genius. Paganini, who had the capacity of a wizard, to rule human passion as he listed, either from the vulgar inclination for notoriety or gain, chose to wed empyricism to power. Not content with the high sovereignty of a mighty artist, to hold a perfect sway over emotion, by cutting antics on a single string, he entered into competition with a dancer on the tight-rope. Men of genius, on other instruments than the violin, have unfortunately been tempted to make that the rule which Paganini made the exception, and to take that for their system, which, with him, was only sport. These men of a true inspiration, capable, if just to that inspiration, of moving souls in their profoundest consciousness, have preferred the wages of ingenuity to the immortality of fame. The noblest art is thus turned into elegant jugglery; and the musician that so degrades it, is, to a cultivated audience, precisely what a conjuror, who can eat fire, or balance a poker on his nose, is to country clowns. True art, to be sure, delights in overcoming difficulties; but it overcomes them for a purpose; and the conquest it uses as a means, but never stops in it as an end.

Within the last two winters I have heard, in common with enraptured crowds, two musicians, who, in the spirit of right enthusiasm, have subdued the obstinacy of a most obstinate instrument. The men I allude to are Knoop and Bohrer, and the instrument is the violencello. Most glorious sounds have they flung upon the winds of Yankee-land, and most devotedly have such of our free and enlightened citizens, as the grace of God has blessed with taste, gone to hear. Both these men are masters, and both are different. Knoop is a zealot, and you cannot but observe his zeal. He is a dogged adorer of his instrument, and he clings to it with ungainly gesture, but with fervid love; onward he careers, in zephyr and in tempest, and rising into ecstasy himself, seems unconscious of the ecstasy he has created. Bohrer is earnest as well as Knoop; but he is earnest with more external grace.

He is perfectly at his ease ; looks blandly towards the
audience, from time to time ; evinces his consciousness
of their sympathy ; throws out his floods of rapture
with a facility that almost appears indolent ; in spright
ly sallies, seems to cheer his instrument with smiles ;
and in pensive passages, hangs over it with a languid
and indulgent fondness. I constantly see things in the
way of analogy ; and after this fashion, regarding the
instruments of these men as their wives, I will show in
what aspect each artist was presented to my vagrant
imagination. Knoop was an inspired rustic, that
clasped his bride and kissed her, and cared not who
was present. Bohrer was a polished and well-bred
gentleman, whose affection was evident, but *comme il
faut* ; in fact, Bohrer, with his loved one, " behaved
himsel afore folk." Yet, with all this apparent ease
and self-possession, his soul was concentred in his
work ; every touch, every movement, contributed to
increase the excitement, or to deepen the impression,
until the brain was giddy to sickness ; until the heart
was full to suffocation.

Glorious, however, as such music is, its effect is by
no means universal. It is too highly artistical for instinctive appreciation. The tones to which the common
heart responds are never elaborate or involved. The
tones to which our most touching associations are

linked, it does not require training to feel. Thence it is, that the music which longest holds its power on us; which earliest begins its influence, and loses its influence the latest; the music which delights our childhood and cheers our age; which the popular memory preserves, and which the popular affections cherish; — this music is always simple. Thus it is with the music of love. Love, being the simplest of sentiments, rejects all but the simplest expression, be this expression in word or tone. The love-lyrics of Burns are among the finest that were ever written, and they are all adapted to old popular tunes, not only familiar, but even homely. Burns, with the instinct of a true poet, saw that whatever a nation preserves for successive generations, is not conventional, but human. Guided by such an instinct, he took up the old airs of his country, and wed them to immortal verse. Carolan, the last of the Irish bards, a man of rare genius and of noble heart, was in melody what Burns was in verse, a production of nature's finest moulding. Moore has given words to many of these airs; but there is small congruity between the words and the airs; the words seem written with the oil of roses, but the airs are as the echoes in lonely caves, or as the breezes over mountain heather.

The music of patriotism is simple. All national airs

are simple. The power of such airs you do not need to
be told.   In father-land, these airs, as you know, can
endow the heart with the bravery of a lion ; in exile
they subdue it to an infant's weakness.   The Swiss, in
foreign armies, you are aware, cannot bear the " Ranz
de Vaches."   The Swiss are not in this peculiar.
What Briton does not feel his heart beat more quickly,
as the swell of his national anthem comes upon his ear ?
I have seen Irishmen aroused almost to madness by a
local melody.   I knew a blind harper, who, after years,
recognized an early friend by the manner in which he
danced to a certain tune.   I have heard of a poor Irish
girl, running into a parlor convulsed in tears, when a
lady was playing one of her native ballads : " O
ma'am ! " she exclaimed, " dear, dear ma'am ! play
that again ! play that again ! O, dear lady, play that !
I love to hear it ! "   These sounds transported, over
distance and years, the spirit of the poor home-sick girl.
She was again in the scenes of her infancy, of her
youth ; the hut where she was born, was before her ;
the parents that reared and blessed her, started to her
view ; her kindred, her playmates, her passages of girl's
love and romance, the tragedy and comedy of her
unsophisticated woman's life, were all summoned in
those pregnant tones.

The music of piety, too, is simple. Simple were

those strains which the early Christians murmured in dens and caves of the earth; simple are those Gregorian chaunts, which the church has since poured out in her triumph and glory; simple is that Miserere, which, if all Christendom could hear, all Christendom would weep; simple is that Stabat Mater, which describes the divinest of women, in the holiest of sorrows; simple were those psalms, and hymns, and godly songs, by which the Scotch raised, among their glens and mountains, in the hard days of persecution, the voice of an honest testimony. This allusion to Scotland, calls to mind a very remarkable effect of simple devotional music, to which I once was witness. The church in which I heard it was not in connection with the Kirk, for it had the advantage of an organ. A young student of the university, on this occasion, played this organ. The first verses of the hymn were hopeful and aspiring, and the youthful artist adapted his modulation to the sentiment with admirable skill. The last stanza was deeply plaintive; without changing the tune, by a rapid turn he altered the manner. The minister and his audience suddenly burst into tears. How many histories of the invisible Spirit, how many secret annals of the heart, how many thoughts of affection, of grief, of penitence, sad recallings of the past, melancholy bodings of the future, did these few touches awaken!

Alas! the minstrel who called them up is now himself but a memory. He has passed from earth; like the sounds which his genius awakened, his life was a transient sweetness, that soon melted into silence. The hand which once had such enchantment in its touch, is now rigid in the palsied grave; the heart, so accordantly strung, has had its living chords dissolved; a lute broken to fragments in the dust, it will no more, to the ear of mankind, discourse most eloquent music.

THE YOUNG MUSICIAN.

I MENTIONED in my last a young musician. I intro-
duce him again, not only from partiality of recollection,
but also because he is connected in my thoughts with
some loiterings and strollings, — a few reminiscences
of which I mean at present to give you.

When my acquaintance commenced with this young
friend, he was a student in the University of Glasgow.
About eighteen years of age, handsome, and of goodly
presence, he was withal a youth of most excellent
spirit. To the refinement of mind, which springs from
liberal studies and good society, he joined the courtesy
of an affectionate nature, and the frankness of an honest
heart. More a musical enthusiast than a scholastic
reader, he loved the divine art with his entire soul ; and
whatever hours he could abstract from his academic
exercises, and whatever money he could spare from his
necessary expenses, he devoted to its cultivation.

My residence for a time was in Greenock; and Greenock, which now by railroad is within an hour's travel of Glasgow, was then about two hours' sail by steamboat. By means of this facility, my young friend had frequent opportunities of pleasant relaxation, and I the privilege of agreeable society. My dwelling was outside the town; and the waves of the beautiful Clyde washed almost the steps of my door. Beyond its ample waters, we could see from my windows the towers of Rosneath, crowning the noble woods which the high-born Campbells had long called theirs; farther in the view arose the Ayrshire mountains, and sublimely over all was spread the many-colored and the many-clouded sky of Scotland. Often were the occasions, and pleasant, when we watched this landscape together, — a landscape that had endless changes, and in every change was glorious. Morning, evening, noon, there was novelty, and when grief was absent, novelty was rapture. Sometimes the sun arose in clearness, and forest, and glen, and mountain, and lake, met the eye in splendor, and filled the heart with joy. But this sun, which came out so fair, often went down in blood-red flame, leaving the tempest and the seas to rage in darkness. We gazed and we admired; but also we felt, that while we gazed and admired, others trembled and wept. The shore had mourning, and the deep destruction ; through the starless arch of heaven were borne the wailings of despair, while death, walking in terror, gave his victims to a fathomless sepulchre, with the shrieking winds above them for a dirge, and the eternal waters around them for a shroud. Sometimes the morning dawned in gloom, with the river merely visible through the sleepy vapors, and the highlands hidden within depths of clouds. But as the day advanced, this curtain of mist would be folded up ; gradually the panorama expanded ; first the plain came out freshly to the light ; the hill-side next appeared, with every hue playing along its heather ; finally, the bare and rocky peaks boldly raised their lofty foreheads in the open azure.

Numerous, also, were the wanderings which we have had in company ; and he who has roamed in Scotland with a congenial friend, has few greater luxuries to regret, and none greater to envy. With most moderate funds, and no ceremony, we had enjoyments which prompted us to pity kings. The hills and the valleys at our threshold were in themselves exhaustless ; and taking a wide circuit, staff in hand and wallet on shoulder, satisfied with coarse fare and rest where we could find it, after a short sojourn we returned to the point whence we set out, not much poorer in purse, and vastly richer in happiness.

Let me sketch a few of these vagrancies for you, as illustrations of humble tourists in search of the picturesque, — no, not in search, but in enjoyment of it.

Once we set out from Greenock, on a summer evening, to walk to Largs. Largs is a village on the border of the Clyde, nearer to its mouth than Greenock, by, I believe, about sixteen miles. Our way lay along the river, widening at every step, until it mingles with the ocean. The atmosphere was so balmy, that it was luxury to live; the horizon was serenely clear, and, except the evening star, there was no speck in the canopy of blue. On our left were the thick-leaved woods, on our right the drowsy river, and, between them both, we jogged on merrily, as to a bridal. In the twinkling of an eye the weather changed, the air darkened, the winds grew loud, the rain fell in torrents, the waters roared to madness, night came, no shelter was at hand, and we were yet some miles from our resting place. We reached the town at last, drenched to the bone, and found a warm shelter in a hospitable inn. We were soon laughing lustily in cosy blankets, extracting pleasure from our pains, with a table between our beds, smoking with hot cakes, hot coffee, and hot cutlets. Willingly, I would take at any time again the same endurance with the same enjoyment.

Sailings on the lakes, we have had also. We have

seen the Trossachs, Lock Katrine, and mused through
the groves of Inverary.   We knew nothing of common-
place and systematic travelling, and all to us was the
freshness of nature, and the romance of tradition.
Inverary, — seat of the great Campbells, — shrouded
in the magic of story, and girded by flood and mountain, was exciting to us, as if a steamboat had never
darkened its waters.   Just as we were entering the
gate, a gentleman went in at the same time, of the
ducal family, who was then on an electioneering expe-
dition in the neighborhood.   I had long desired to see
a Highland gentleman in native costume, and as I went
into the hall of Inverary Castle I was fully gratified.
Campbell of Islay was standing there in full array,
with kilt and dirk, bonnet and plume, and the tartan of
his clan.   He was all that a chieftain should be — of
manly appearance, of chivalric courtesy, and of hospitable speech.   Changed as society has been by modern
revolution — and in much changed for the better — the
costume which this gentleman assumed, when his desire
was to ingratiate sympathy, evinced how long old-world
notions dwell in the popular affection, even when they
have vanished from the popular theory.   Fact it is, that
nations, as they grow in age, exist like individuals in
the past ; and though the advance of years be often in
both an advance towards idiocy and decay, the mere

instinct of life renders the past proportionately more precious. Fact it also is, that whatever be our logic, our feelings are conservative, and our logic has no power, until a goading pressure has entirely reversed our feelings.

Bodily, you were never, I apprehend, in Scotland; much, doubtless, you have been there in spirit; for you have read — as who have not? — Scott and Burns. I will show you, however, what in reality may be done in the way of touring in no great number of hours. After an early breakfast one day, my young friend and myself departed from Greenock: we sailed up Loch Gair to Arrochar; from Arrochar we crossed a few miles to Tarbolton; passed from that point to the head of Loch Lomond; sailed down on the other side to Roadinnan, where we stopped for the night at the foot of Ben Lomond. Rising at dawn, we climbed the mountain, and met the sun upon his summit. Descending from the celestial to the earthly, we did ample justice to a Scottish breakfast — and, even at this distance of time and space, I can honestly testify that Dr. Johnson has not overpraised it.

The scenery, as we again embarked on the lake, appeared lovelier than before; for it is indeed wonderful, how a hearty meal brightens the face of creation. Never, if you can possibly avoid it, let hunger beset

you in an excursion amidst the beautiful. It is worse
than fog, cloud, rain — either separately or all together.
It is a foul fiend, which sun, stars, hills or glades can
soothe into no complacency. It banishes the smile of
pleasure, and it silences the laugh of mirth. I have
noticed a company grow dull and sullen amidst scenery
fair as Eden. This insidious demon was amongst them;
and it was not until the wretch was banished, by the
powerful charm of a massive loaf, that the scales fell
from the eyes of his victims.

To return, however, to our tour. Quitting the foot
of Ben Lomond, the steamer carried us to Balloch, the
extremity of the lake on the low land side. Our travel
then lay by Leven Water, until we reached Dumbarton,
from which another steamer took us on to Greenock.
Within a circle, which may thus be traversed in a day,
we passed through a succession of scenes, glorious to
the sight, but more glorious to the fancy — inspiring
from variety of objects, but more inspiring from wealth
of association. When from the pinnacle of Ben Lomond I looked down on the islet-speckled lake that lay
at his base in sunny sleep, or around on the wild wilderness of hills and waters, my imagination began to work,
and it was solitude no longer, for it became peopled by
the witcheries of Scott. The poetry of Smollet came
with the evening breeze that played on Leven Water;

and the memory of his genius, by his native streams, made that stream sacred in pensive thought, as we gazed on the shadow of his monument in its placid brightness. And, while leaning over the precipice of Dumbarton, the moral sublimity of the patriot and martyr-hero, Wallace, to whom its castle gave a dungeon, was more exciting to us than the material sublimity of the sombre rock on which the castle stands.

Will you allow me to intrude on you the recollection of one ramble ? I had decided on a visit to Edinburgh, and take in my way a loiter through the vale of Clyde. My friend wished to bear me company as far as Lanark. I reached Glasgow in the afternoon, and found him ready to join me ; but, unfortunately, the stage-coach, which was the last for the day, had only one vacant place, and as I had an engagement next morning on the way, that I was obliged to secure. I went on, therefore, without him. It was a fine autumn evening ; the sun glanced gaily along the river, which here is within narrow banks, and dashes on sportively in rustic buoyancy. The hard smooth road, upon which previous rains had laid the dust, was gemmed on each border with cheerful cottages ; luxuriant orchards, burdened with fruit, hung over its sides ; the horses pranced away proudly and speedily ; the driver gossipped by turns with his passengers and with his steeds ; nameless jest and hearty laughter hastened the time and shortened the journey, until I found myself at the place where I was to quit the coach. From this I was to take a by-way to a village on the hills. Lovely are these by-ways of Britain; lovely their hawthorn hedges, trellised with ivy and honey-suckle; lovely their shade and solitude — their wild flowers and their birds — their perfumed banks for the traveller's repose, and their warbling concerts for his solace. The twilight was on the verge of darkness, when I entered the hamlet at which I was to rest. I had fixed myself in the parlor of its quiet inn, and was musing over a stiff cup of tea, when, to my surprise and pleasure, my friend bolted into the room. He had crossed the country on foot, and enthusiasm bore him on without fatigue, charmed by the new phases of beauty which opened to his view at every step. An hour's chat, and then to sleep, with the stillness of nature around us, deep enough to keep a Cockney awake.

When an early hour the next morning found us again upon the road, we proposed to breakfast with a farmer, to whom I had an introduction, and whose residence was a few miles distant on our way. The head-man of the place, whose acquaintance I had the privilege to make, came to escort us beyond the borders, and to do the honors of his village. This head-man was the shopkeeper of the place, a dispenser of most complicated merchandise, from pins to reaping-hooks, from thimbles to plough-shares, with a goodly assortment of hams and harrows, of gimcracks and gingerbread, of hogs' lard and primers, of soap and psalm books. He was the grandee of the neighborhood, the speculator, the capitalist, the man of wealth and wisdom, a combined epitome of Rothschild and Solomon. He put on his hat with dignity, buttoned his coat with satisfaction, walked with measured pace, shook his head with profound sagacity, and intimated the possession of a marvellous knowledge by his pauses. When we had attained the summit of some rising ground that overlooked the village, he turned round, folded his arms, and remained some moments in eloquent silence. A fine contemplative serenity marked the expression of his features, as he surveyed the sphere of his mercantile activity and his social consequence. There it was, flooded with the lustre of the morning sun, about a half a mile beneath us, and no corner of it concealed : a score of low thatched cabins on one side, "all in a row," and a score to match them, "all in a row," on the other. This architectural uniformity was elegantly relieved by two houses, which had each a second story — one the tavern, and the other belonging to our venerable friend.

After a while, he addressed himself to me, with most imposing gravity : " Wonderful times these, sir." " Yes, verily," answered I. " Wonderful times, sir. All things going by steam, sir. Even babies grow faster now than when I was a bairn. Great times for knowledge and improvement. We've come on a bit here, I can tell you, sir. Would you believe it, sir, but thirty years ago there was not a dozen houses in that town, and see, sir, what it is now ! " He seemed quite elated in pointing to this remarkable illustration of rapid progress. ". But we know how to do things here, sir ; we're an enterprising people, sir, that we are. We don't get on I ken, so quick as the Glasgow folks; but in our own way, sir, we manage matters to please ourselves : we're steady and sure, that we are." " Though," said I, " you have no foreign commerce, I suppose you've an extensive domestic business ? " " We've our share, sir," and he shook his noddle. " You don't happen to sell," I inquired, " any Kilmar-nock night-caps ?" " No, sir, no, sir ; they're a drug here : we can knit night-caps ourselves, sir — it's a branch of native trade. We're concerned a bit in the egg business, and we're about to form a joint live chicken company ; it'll be a handsome speck, sir. We've a building company, and we hope by and by to have an assurance office : I've a small investment in the building, and I'll give them a decent penny towards the insurance affair. Sound to the bone here, sir. Capital well vested, sir — good return, sir. Nothing like spirit, sir. What's a man, what's a community without spirit ? Nothing, sir, nothing ; you could'nt do better, sir, than settle among us — a growing place, on the high road to prosperity. We intend soon to light our town with gas — finest coal for gas here in the world, and we're talking of having a gas company." This was too much — it was not in humanity to keep down cachinnation ; so, pleading haste, I bade him a rapid good morning, and saved my reputation.

Having reposed a few hours with our farmer host, and partaken of his hospitable fare, a leisurely stroll brought us in the afternoon to Lanark. The farmer came with us, and did not leave us until he consigned us to a brother of his for the night. Though in the humble occupation of a carrier, this brother had a house that was the perfection of neatness, and his wife and himself were the perfection of good nature. Our supper was from a board covered with homely plenty. We slept in compact little chambers, with beds and windows curtained in the purest white ; and we arose to a breakfast, at which we had trout, which were that morning caught in a contiguous stream. The scenery around Lanark is inexpressibly lovely, and the falls of

Clyde, with more beauty than sublimity, to any one who has seen Niagara, yet, like all cataracts, defy description.

But, though I cannot describe to you the torrent, or the woodland paradise in which it is embosomed, I can tell you something of a young blacksmith, who was my voluntary and unpaid guide. At the upper fall, we sat in a rustic bower ; we listened to the roar of waters, and watched the tumbling flood, which seemed, as its broken gushings mingled with the sun-beams, a shower of gems and rain-bows. Romance is in all conditions ; and in every condition the poetry of the heart has purity and exaltation. While I was admiring this summer aspect of the fall, the blacksmith dwelt on some of its winter appearances. He used to see it, when the frost congealed its brilliant driblets on the rocks, and when the moon poured her splendor upon the forest and the fall. And one used to see it with him ; and here was the charm. In this bower he came to meet his ladye-love ; and here they mingled the outpourings of affection with the voice of song ; and she, who was then a gladsome lassie, was now a youthful matron. Very oddly, had they heard Rossini's music, or read Bulwer's novels, they could not have courted with more romance, or been fonder of sylvan shades for their whisperings. But nature, after all, is the greatest teacher. Young man and maiden, royal or rustic, may differ in expression, but in little else ; for nature, which is no monopolist, is not in the texture of the garment, but in the living pulse that throbs beneath it. This young pair, as well as the most refined of aristocrats, would woo in silence and alone ; they sought the moon-light and the grove, and here they had a trysting place, which Queen Mab herself might choose, if she had an elfin lover ; but no doubt the anthem of the eternal cataract, that rushed beside and beneath them, was a faint sound, while they breathed their mutual vows ; and the vista between hills to the far-off sky, and the gleaming of stars upon the dancing waters, were little heeded in the reflection of love in meeting eyes. Wherever nature can act in freedom, life in its essential has much of equality ; the worst anomalies of life arise from the paralysis of nature by sordid destitution, or the perversion of nature by artificial desires.

The truth of these remarks had practical illustration in another, but very opposite kind of person, whom I came across in this neighborhood, and on this evening. A few nights previously, I had been in the theatre in Glasgow, and was profoundly affected by the pathos which a young performer threw into his acting. He was, as I found upon inquiry, a person of some genius, but of no discretion. He once had highest prospects on the London boards — was admired by the elder Kean, and at his recommendation procured an excellent engagement. But drinking and dissipation ruined all. In the foam of the goblet all high aspiration was drowned, ambition quenched, and hope forever darkened. He not only neglected his studies, but forgot his appointments, and when he ought to have been in the green-room, was insensible in the tavern. The result is clear: confidence was taken from him, and he was cast upon the world with pitiless contempt. Now and then a provincial manager would have him in a favorite part, and on such occasions needed all precautions to keep him sober.

On the evening that I was in Lanark, I saw, by bills through the town, that he was to give recitations, and I went to hear them. The place, I think, was an old market-house. The elocutionist came from behind a sort of screen. His face was pale and pimpled, his eyes heavy, his graceful person clad in vesture that was as worn as himself. His boots were patched, his trousers brushed to thin elemental threads, and his coat buttoned closely to the chin. He was accompanied by a female, already passée in age and beauty ; her dress was tawdry, rouge was stuck upon her pallid and withered features. She took part in some dialogue pieces, and was affectation, vanity, and poverty, personified. The gentleman, although he seemed to have taken some strong drink, recited with exceeding truthfulness and force, and with a simplicity that combined fine perception with high culture. But to whom did he recite ? Besides my young friend and myself, there were two factory girls — three men, in soiled fustian jackets — half a dozen young scamps, that yelled like wolves or jackalls — a dandy, that kept his hat on, and sucked the head of his cane, and an old crimson-nosed toper, that snored after the first five minutes, to the close of the performance. The weary and wretched speaker retired from this beggarly bundle of auditors without enough to pay for the dirty tallow candles, which dropped their grease upon the floor, and made the darkness both dismal and visible. And thus, while this man of genius was a ruined outcast, without friendship or funds, by means of inordinate passions and disordered will, a humble mechanic, by moderate wants and unsophisticated affection, had secured all the pleasures which wisdom can seek, or which earth can bestow — the blessings of health, competence, love, and home.

At Lanark, my young friend and I separated ; he returned to Glasgow, and I went on to Edinburgh. Once again I saw him. He was going home to Eng-

land to spend the vacation.   He was in the the heyday
of life and hope ; already the gladness that awaited his
return, was before him in anticipation ; the clasp of his
father's hand, and the pressure of his mother's bosom ;
the merry welcome of his brothers and sisters, and the
hearty greetings of his school-day companions.   He
arrived to enjoy all that he had anticipated, but he did
not enjoy it long.   From an evening circle of mirth
and gaiety, he came away loaded with fever, and died,
after an illness of two days.   As his image often comes
to me in the recollections, that people the summer
twilight or the winter interval, between the closing of
the shutters and the lighting of the candles, I could
not omit a reminiscence of him, from the individual
musings which these scribblings are intended to record.

Edinburgh, the beautiful and the far-famed, I mention only for the sake of a little incident.   Lions, I like
well to see, and I saw them ; but they have been described to the extremity of a hair and the point of a
claw.   I have nothing to add to these zoological
researches ; and truth to say, if I had the ability, I
want the inclination.   The most agreeable hour I spent
was with Mr. Steele, then a young sculptor of eminent
promise ; promise which he has since fulfilled.   The
stamp of an artist was on his pale and thoughtful coun-

tenance ; his mere gestures and expression had a grace which evinced an innate perception of the fair and the fit. Like every man of a true inspiration, he was modest and courteous. He led me through his studio ; showed me works in different stages, from embryo thoughts, rudely fashioned into clay, to those which stood completely embodied in the full maturity of chiselled marble. Sculpture, I ventured to observe, was the most perfect manifestation of ideal beauty through material form. He seemed pleased with the remark ; merely, I suppose, because it implied a desire to judge of his art with a rational appreciation. I went from his door, confident of his progress. I had no critical skill ; I could give no reason for the faith that was in me ; but the faith was there, and it has been since justified. A few minutes after quitting his door, I was seated in a canal packet boat, making all speed back to Glasgow. One other passenger was in it, and that was a young lady. The circumstance justified conversation without an introduction, and ere long we were deep in gossip about things in general, and Edinburgh in particular. I mentioned my visit to Mr. Steele, and gave hearty utterance to the feelings which it inspired. " I, sir," said she, " am Mr. Steele's sister." Pleasant it was to me, that my words were not words of censure ; pleasant to me afterwards, was the memory of this praise; and flowing honestly and warmly as it did from a stranger's lips to a sister's ear, I would fain hope that to the lady herself it was also pleasant. I would not for the critical powers of Longinus, and the opulent wit of Rabelais, have wounded that young girl's feelings; and yet, unconsciously, I might have stung them to the quick. Mr. Steele has recently been selected by Sir Robert Peel to execute one of three great national works.

Thus the stream of years flows on, sweeping some to oblivion, and carrying others to the open day of fame. But, after all, this course is only comparative. The most noted will sink at last with the most obscure. My young friend awakened a few tones of emotion within the circle of a span, and then came silence. The Scottish sculptor has made for his conceptions lasting habitations in solid forms. Yet had my young friend an imagination as mighty in harmony as Handel's, he would, notwithstanding, be forgotten; and had the Scottish sculptor the plastic chisel of Phidias, a like destiny would also be his. The statues of Greece are in ashes, and the music of Zion has not left an echo. Time not only wears out arts, but ultimately it will alter nature. Not only the sound of the lute and the lyre die, but so will the sound of the wind and the wave; the colors of the pencil fade, so will the glory of the sun ; the sculptured marble moulders, so will the mountain from which it was hewn. The only immortality is Thought, and that which thought inhabits — Spirit.

A DAY IN SPRINGFIELD.

———◆———

FOR the first time in my life, I have been to-day in an American cotton mill. I went through it, and surveyed both its living, and its inanimate machinery. I have been through mills of most huge dimensions in England, of which this one seemed to me a bright and elegant miniature edition. The gigantic vastness of an English mill is more imposing, but the superior cleanness of an American mill is more pleasing. Hordes of children pant wearily in an English mill; in an American one, but few children are employed. Fewer men, also, are engaged in American cotton factories. The principal operatives, therefore, in American cotton factories, are young girls. They come to these factories from all parts of the country in New England; are daughters of farmers; many of them well educated, and most of them of excellent character. After a few years of hard work, they return, and marry on the strength of their earnings. In the mills they are decently dressed, and on holidays, they are the gayest of the gay. In looks, they are generally pretty; in appearance, healthy; in demeanor, modest and retiring. One evil in American factories corresponds to a like one in those of England; and that is, long hours of labor. Here I find that work commences with the light, and closes, at the present season, at six. In summer time it commences at five in the morning, and closes only at seven in the evening. An hour and a half each day, I believe, is allowed for meals. I have, myself, a theory against factories, in their most mitigated operations; but as, with our civilization, so many fellow creatures are likely to be engaged in them, I trust that facts may prove my theory false. That much may be effected to render such labor consistent with all that is best in the development of human nature, the literary productions of the Lowell factory girls evince; and where much has been done, there may be more. Girls from England and Canada, I found, had been enlisted into work in the mills here; and although the managers discovered that some of them were rather rebellious creatures, others were highly appreciated, for peaceful and docile industry. Factories, I know, must be, and as they must, let them be as consistent with the happiness of their laborious workers, as every human effort can make them. But as it is, there are few modes of occupation that give me less pleasurable emotions, than these immense combinations of throbbing engines and throbbing hearts. Our civilization has its foundation in terrific sacrifices; for all our material enjoyments, our systematic comforts, there are piles and piles of victims, one grade treading down another, and standing on it — from the pinnacle of privilege and pleasure, down to the depths of hopeless ignorance and ceaseless toil.

"Disguise thyself as thou wilt, still slavery thou art a bitter draught," and, in my opinion, slavery to machinery is not the least bitter draught in the cup of servitude.

While waiting in the sitting parlor of · the hotel, previous to supper, an elderly man of very marked appearance was my only companion. His face was oval, of beautiful contour; his white hair combed back from a forehead of noble height, his eye benignant, but piercing. His conversation — for we had conversation — was calm, intelligent, singularly correct and elegant in phraseology. I am not given to the superstition that you may know a remarkable man by his forehead or his nose, and yet I was impressed by this man. I had, one way or the other, an idea that he was somebody. We went together to the supper-room.

He ate very slightly, and then left the table. A gentleman, who remained after him, asked me, " Do you know who that is ? " " No," I replied ; " but I have been peculiarly struck by him." " That," said my fellow-guest, " is Mr. Audubon." " What ! Mr. Audubon, the celebrated American ornithologist ? " " The same." I spoke most sincerely, when I replied, " there is no man in the United States, whom I am more pleased to see than Mr. Audubon." On our return to the parlor, Mr. Audubon gratified us by showing some magnificent prints of a grand new work, he is about to publish, on the Quadrupeds of America. It would be vain for me to try to give you, by description, an idea of the vigor and the life which appear in these drawings ; the grace of their positions, and in many instances, the exquisite comicry of their looks. When Mr. Audubon had kindly done all this, he set out to travel in the stage coach for hours in the night, through a deluge of rain, and roads compounded of mud and ice. Mr. Audubon is one of the most distinctive instances of the union of enthusiasm with patience, of genius with labor. His devotion to his favorite pursuit has been as unremitting as it has been fervid ; through travel, fatigue, danger, he has still preserved the glow of his soul and the tenor of his way. Years ago in England, Professor Wilson and other men of poetic fire, admired the enthusiast of the woods, with his black hair, and his bold front — such was the character; it has not since changed; true, his locks have grown hoary, and wrinkles have crept into his face; but his eye has not become dim, nor his natural force abated. With other attributes of genius he has its disinterestedness. By his first great work, he lost twenty-five thousand dollars; there is a smaller edition, by which his friends hope this loss may be refunded. Yet, although pecuniary loss ought not, in this case as others, to be the fate of genius, to say nothing of toil and trouble, still, what noble compensation in high thoughts and a living name! Such compensation, at least, Mr. Audubon has; but the world should not make that his all. Have you ever read Professor Wilson's eloquent article on him in Blackwood? If not, read it.

The next morning, being considerably fatigued, I was late for the common breakfast; and with whom think you did I get mine? Why, with three Judges of the Supreme Court, and a bar of the most eminent lawyers in the State,* and among the most eminent in the nation. They were here in special session on an exciting case of murder. I went with them into court; remained there all the forenoon; came out, dined, and

---

* **Massachusetts.**

then again returned. The matter, of course, will be to you scarcely worth relation, except that it was my first time of being present at a capital trial in America, and there may be some small interest in the vividness of new and contrasted impressions. Although in a country town, the court room was more neat, more clean, and more comfortable, than any that I have ever seen in Ireland or England. The judges went from their lodgings in the order of age, preceded by the sheriff, and took their seats gravely on the bench. Let me tell you, that, notwithstanding all my early associations, I did not miss the parade or the robings. Indeed, I think my feelings were more solemn without them. There was something, indeed, that almost awed me in the spectacle of three plainly dressed men, having a controling influence on the life of a fellow creature, sustained in their authority by the free opinion of those around them, and the sense of justice ; having no other grandeur than that which lies in learning, wisdom, integrity, and years. Nor was the audience less impressive to me, in its decorum, silence, and submission ; obedient to the predominant sentiment of law, by which alone a community can have either civilization or security. The progress of evidence developed complications of crime. A man was killed who had made one of a gang to tear down a house. The house had been subject to some odium; the inmates had fled; a lawless band, it would seem, was made a ruffian the less, by one who was as great a ruffian as himself. Having continued through the day, the scene apppeared to me specially dramatic by candle light. The three judges, with their serious faces, seemed yet more solemn in the dim gleam of the tapers. The members of the bar, not engaged in examination, are listening with fixed attention, or musing in concentrative abstraction. The prisoner sits within a railing exactly opposite to the bench. He is a man respectable in station, and fifty years of age. As the candles faintly glimmer over his features, they seem sad, thoughtful, worn, and not ungentle. I could not avoid thinking what a contrast that face now presented, in the hour of retribution, to its hour of passion; how different that despondent eye, from that which had been shot with glaring vengeance; how different that arm, relaxed in weariness, from that which was nerved to plunge the murderous dagger in a human heart. And this man, who unsluiced the fountain of his brother's life, had home and kindred, and, doubtless, all the affections that belong to such relations; and these were at this moment around him with most devoted anxiety. Three brothers sat outside the bar. The prisoner was the eldest; and the arrangement was an ascending progression from a fine young man in the bloom of life, to the individual whose fate they awaited. His son-in-law, a beginner, as I understood, in the legal profession, was indefatigable in aiding the counsel for his defence. Scarcely is there any evil, which leaves us solitary in this earth of kindred humanities; and scarcely is there any sin so dark, as to rob us of sympathy, from some heart that has bonds with ours.

There is no place in which human passions are so revealed, as in a court of justice. In political assemblies they are but partial; in those of worship, they are suppressed; on the stage they are only feigned; in the court alone, they are various, and they are real. I must except the lawyers, for they have the simulation of actors without their art. But for the rest; observe the audience. Take your place near the bench, and look up towards the opposite gallery. Contemplate that dense mass of countenances, of every age, and each with characteristic and earnest expression. There is one man about the middle of the group; he is so crushed by those behind, that he has to lean his elbows on the front rail, and place his face between his hands. His coat is a rusty drab and patched, his cuffs are greasy, and the face between them is a study for Cruikshank! See when he closes his lips, how the wrinkles converge towards his mouth; each wrinkle contains a grin, but no one of the grins has a streak of humor or of light. See him, now, when he opens his mouth — in the fore part of it, two upper teeth are wanting; his widened face is grotesque, but not funny; it is odd, but you cannot laugh at it; it is one of those countenances in a thousand, which fixes your attention, not by attraction but compulsion; which you do not exactly fear, which you do not exactly hate; which does not command your esteem, nor yet move your contempt; which, beholding once, you can never forget; but which you never desire to behold again. Then where, as well as in a court of justice, will you observe suspense, grief, terror, despair, so truly, so tragically, depicted? this scene of all the passions in their consummation and retribution, the winding up of those doings, whose ways are misery, and whose end is death.

Scenes similar to this, and yet different from it, in other lands, passed across my memory. One especially occurred to me, of a trial, at which I was present, in the south of Ireland. It was a trial for murder. This was now the night of the third day. Even the bench and the bar were but feebly lighted, and the body of the court had only such a glimmer, as a wretched tallow candle here and there afforded. The jury have retired. The judge, a venerable old man, has folded his crimson robe around his breast, and reclines back exhausted. The lawyers are some engaged in low whispers, others are in postures of listlessness and fatigue. The prisoner — what of him ? There he is, unhappy creature ! behind an inner railing. A policeman stands on each side of his barrier, and from each side the rays of a flickering candle pass athwart his features — and what features ! Look at them — his low forehead, with no stamp of thought ; his eye, with no dawn of speculation ; his hard, weather-tanned cheek ; his mouth large, coarse, thick, which bespeaks nothing but the animal. And there he stands, stolid, unmoved, impassive ; now, his poor unmeaning face turns towards the audience, now to the judge ; then toward the jury box ; never with any concern, except, that it had occasionally a look of stupid and puzzled wonder, which appeared to say, what's all this about ? Then, the audience. The old man, whose son was, perhaps, next day for trial, and the stalwart peasant from the fields, waiting to be a witness for his brother or his neighbor. The elder matron to leave the town, it may be, childless, and be dragged down with her gray hairs in sorrow to the grave. The young maiden — a few weeks since, blooming as summer's freshest rose, now pale in apprehension for her brother or her betrothed. These, surrounded by a mass of

faces, stamped with want, with suffering, or with vice ;
all intent, fixed, eager — formed a spectacle as wild
and gaunt, as the gloomy and sublime Salvator ever
fancied or ever painted.　An hour passes away ; eyes
wander from the accused to the door that conceals the
weighers of his destiny.　It stirs — the heart leaps — it
opens, and they come forth in solemn order.　This
dense silent crowd have all now but one soul, that soul
but one thought, and that thought an awful suspense.
The question is put : Guilty or not guilty ?　The
answer is, Guilty !　Had the prisoner changed color,
had he shed tears, had he evinced any intelligent
heroism, I would have been relieved !　But no ! the
poor, forlorn, mindless victim, did not seem to think
that these matters had any relation to him.　The judge
placed the black cap on his head, addressed him in
gentle and moving tones, and then pronounced the
sentence, that made every heart quake, and every
knee tremble.　Exhortation and sentence were alike
in vain ; they found no response of either compunction
or dread ; they did not enkindle or moisten the leaden
eye which still stared unheeding.　Seldom is the terrible doom of the law pronounced in an Irish court,
without the echo of breaking hearts, to whom the
victim of the law is dear.　But about this unfriended
and outcast man, there seemed no shelter of kindred

affections. Had I heard the sobs of a father, the shrieks of a mother, the mad lamentations of a wife, my pity had been softened by a touch of comfort; but this uncheered, unbroken desolation upon the lot of a brother, in my humanity, did not so much move me, as oppress me. Miserable, unimpressed, dogged, he retired with the officials to his prison, and in a few days that miserable creature was hanged ; the life was taken which he had been never taught to use ; and the gallows became the sovereign remedy for the ills of an unprotected infancy, a neglected youth, and a guilty manhood.

Thus I have given you the incidents and impressions of a day, which forms somewhat of a rambling medley, but if the record affords you the least pleasure, it will not have been made in vain.

CHATTERTON.

WHY is it, can you tell me, why so many poets should be from the poor? Most poets have arisen from conditions of life, which were not burdened with wealth. Many things, from time to time, as I reflect on the fact, suggest themselves to me, as the cause of it; but I cannot say that I have ever satisfied myself about it, nor am I much concerned. It might be said, poetry is the language of fancy; and genius, which is not made gross by the riches of the world, can use this language best. Poetry is also the language of struggle; and genius, beset with sordid embarrassments, utters it with all the depth of its tragedy. Poetry is the language of passion; the opulent exhaust passion, but indigent genius idealizes it. Poetry is the language of aspiration; and genius, stimulated by its own wants, and moved by sympathy for those of others, constantly sighs for a condition of existence more perfect than that in which it lives. But it is vain to theorize ; for if one wrote a folio volume of speculation on the point — which he might easily do — the fact would be all the same. From the ranks of lowly life, some of the greatest poets, who have adorned ancient or modern literature, have come forth — not alone to sing the simple songs of the poor, but to tell the tales of heroes and of gods. Tradition — whether true or fabulous — represents Homer, the father of bards, as not over-burdened with the world's goods. Hesiod was a peasant. Virgil was a small farmer ; and he thought it no profanation to defy an emperor, who did not drive him from his poor inheritance. Horace was the son of a Roman freedman and tax-gatherer. Terence had been a slave. Vulgar report represented Shakspeare as a poacher. Ben Jonson was a bricklayer. Taylor, a famous fellow in his day, was a waterman. Allan Ramsay, spent a portion of his life in wig-making ; and I am not sure but he also did something at shaving. Burns held the plough. Hogg tended sheep. And poor Chatterton was the son of a schoolmaster.

The name of Chatterton is well known, and is likely to be long remembered, both for his misfortunes and his his genius. He was born in November, 1752. His birth was in orphanage ; and his death, like his birth, was desolate. Educated at a charity-school, that wonderful boy became a puzzle to hoary scholars. His first years were spent in the drudgeries of an attorney's office. One of his earliest efforts was on the opening of a new bridge in Bristol, when he produced an account of the friars in former times passing over the olden bridge. The fabrication evinced astonishing invention; and this was by a boy of sixteen years of age. The professed discovery of certain old English poems by Chatterton, occurred in this wise: In the church of St. Mary Radcliffe, Bristol, were some six or seven chests of old parchment. Chatterton asserted that among these he found poems by an ancient priest, named Thomas Rowley, and printed a few of his pretended discoveries in the periodicals of the day; but with no pecuniary result. He had left Bristol in the meantime, given up his legal apprenticeship, and was pacing the streets of London, helpless and unfriended, but full of hopes and youth. He transmitted some MSS. to Horace Walpole. The Epicurean Cynic took no notice of them. The poet re-demanded them: the great man returned them with contempt. The great man's contempt was retorted by the poet's indignation. The great man did not dine the worse: unhappily, the poor poet did not dine at all. Mr. Gray and Mr. Mason at once knew Chatterton's MSS. to be forgeries: the wretched youth went on obstinately maintaining the authenticity of Rowley's poems, and was all the while dying of hunger. He labored incessantly; he filled the magazines with noble and heart-burning poetry; but the charmer found none that would keep alive that voice of glorious enchantment — and in a moment of despair, it was quenched forever. Chatterton destroyed himself in passionate destitution, and earned for himself the grave of the Excommunicated. Yet such, to the last, was his kindness for his friends, that, while a gleam of expectation remained, his letters were encouraging, — and he sustained a cheerful tone, when his soul had become dark as " Erebus." I do not think a more affecting incident occurs in the history of English literature, than that of poor Chatterton writing excellent letters to his friends, when he was starving in London. There were times when he wanted a dinner — occasions, when he had not tasted food for twenty-four hours; yet, as if to assure his sister, he would send her a cheap, but delicate present. Such also was the proud sensibility of his nature, that, when walking the streets of London, with famine tearing at his vitals, he was in the habit of refusing invitations to dinner, which he well knew were given from compassion. Once, and once only, he was prevailed on to await supper — and then his enjoyment of it evinced the instinctive voracity which accompanies the last degree of starvation. With a horrid despair thus gathering over him, partly, it must be admitted, brought on by his own proud dishonesty, he became his own self-avenger. The cup of life had become bitter to his taste, and to end the draught, he mingled arsenic with its ingredients. Coleridge exclaims:

> "O! Chatterton, that thou wast still alive,
> Sure thou wouldst spread thy canvass to the gale,
> And love with us the tinkling team to drive
> O'er peaceful freedom's undivided dale —
> And we at sober eve would round thee throng,
> Hanging enraptured on thy stately song —
> And greet with smiles the young-eyed poesy,
> All deftly masked as hoar antiquity."

The arguments for and against the authenticity of Rowley's poems are now of little interest. Such as they are, however, they may be simply, and very briefly stated. Against the authenticity, it is said, that Chatterton produced but few verses of pretended original MSS — whereas, if he had many such treasures, he would have been proud to show them; the likelihood that from an early love of antiquarian lore, his genius would have taken this course; the confession of poor Chatterton himself, that he had written one piece at least, which appeared in the counterfeit style; the probabilty that he, who could write one, could write more; the knowledge of an intimate acquaintance, who was aware that he had blackened and disfigured parchments, that he had sent to the printer's for old MSS.; the evidence of another friend, who traced in Chatterton's conversation, and in the pretended poems of Rowley, the same tone and the same ideas; the variation of the hand-writing of the pieces; the absence of any allusion to Rowley in contemporaneous documents; the want of faults in the poems themselves, which belong to the times in which they profess to have been written; the anachronisms of incident or reference; the inconsistencies of measure and of language; the imitations of subsequent writers : — all these are alleged as sufficient to convict Chatterton of fabrication and imposition.

On the other side are urged : Chatterton's love of fame, which, if he had written such poems, would impel him to claim the glory; his own repeated assertions, and his adherence to such assertions; the short time which he had to produce such a quantity of MSS.; the `allusion to facts and customs; the use of ancient words, in no dictionaries at Chatterton's command :— these, with most abortive attempts to answer positive arguments, make the sum of all that can be said in favor of Rowley's authenticity and Chatterton's honesty.

We thus find Chatterton in the paradoxical position of giving up his honesty to lose that personal fame, which so many barter honesty to acquire.

I am not about to enter on a specific criticism of his works, but merely to revert to such memories, as half-forgotten reading may suggest. " Ella, a tragical Interlude," is a stately drama, of English thought and phraseology, wanting in passion and incident, but having uncommon poetic beauty. In the " Parliament of Sprites," we have a wild and luxurious fertility of antique and descriptive poetry ; that which revels in the past of Britain — that in which Shakspeare found scenery for his " Midsummer Night's Dream" — that in which Memory and Imagination meet and rejoice together. I do not know any other land, where the rural sentiment is so strong as it is in England. The habits of the people seem from the first to have wedded them to nature ; and the nature to which they were familiar was of that middle order between the gentle and the gigantic, which best nurtures the rural sentiment. We find accordingly, this sentiment to be the ruling one in their sports ; the sentiment which trained them to archery, which placed their amusements on the green-sward, or amidst the woodlands — which made the wild free forest the very Paradise of their desire. The sentiment is immortalized in Robin Rood, in his man John, and such other green-wood outlaws. This sentiment overflows, therefore, in every grade of English poetry : in ballad, song, drama, ode and epic. Chatterton evinces that sympathy with the luxuriance of rural imagery, which belongs to the poetry, native to his country, and especially to the best of its earlier verses. " Wharncliff" is one of his finest antique counterfeits. It is wild and romantic in the highest degree ; it displays immense force and imagination, and a great range of poetical expression. " Bothwell " is a story, dark, dismal and pitiful. Both parties of disputants as to Mary of Scotland's guilt or innocence, may quarrel until Doomsday ; but none of them could turn from this affecting story, without being charmed by its interest and pathos. We have the savage warrior, after years of captivity and madness, dismayed, at intervals of sanity, by terrible glancings of memory, which reveal his beautiful " ladye-love," as she was seen in the pride of her loveliness, and then bring his intellect back to the present, to survey the cold Norwegian dungeon, where he bears the chains of a wild beast. We see the giant both of courage and of sin, brought down to child-like meekness, and weeping away his hours in sorrow and in darkness. We see the strong and wicked soul borne to the naked ground, prostrate on the bare bosom of our common mother,

sobbing in broken tones of grief.   We see the strong
and wicked soul, which had feared no crime, of blood,
or guilt, or wrong, melted and humbled by thoughts of
hours to be his no more ; by recollections of his Mary,
exceedingly lovely, and exceedingly loved — guilty, it
may be, but whom all wish to believe innocent ; guilty,
it may be, but yet having such grace and sweetness,
that her errors are forgotten, and a civilized humanity
remains always her advocate.   Chatterton has developed the moving and romantic elements both of character and situation, in this poem, with a force of
emotion, and a felicity of diction, that made me sad,
as' I closed the book, to think what our literature had
lost in the glorious and inspired boy.   Chatterton
evinced how mighty his genius was, by the distance
at which it anticipated experience.   Why, when most
of our boys are but blubbering their books, this super-
human youth was pouring out the thoughts, that swell
and shake the breast of manhood.   Still, there is no
means by ,which genius can altogether anticipate
experience.   The faculties most powerful, therefore,
in the youth of genius, are those which , distinguish
the writings of Chatterton.   These are luxuriance of
fancy, and opulence of expression.   The fancy of
Chatterton is not only rich but strong ; it has not only
a plumage of dazzling splendor, but a pinion of daring

flight; and his language reflects, perfectly, the brilliancy of his fancy, and sustains him amidst the bravest of its soarings. In the genius of Chatterton there are equal precocity and power, a supernatural wildness and a fearful grandeur. In some respects, Chatterton resembled Shelley; in others, he was as dissimilar as possible. Shelley lavished his genius on the future, and Chatterton spent his upon the past. Both of them were zealots; Shelley for phantoms, and Chatterton for forgeries; Shelley, for visions, which he believed were some time to be; Chatterton, for a fable, which he was conscious never had been. A solitary peculiarity attaches to unhappy Chatterton, which leaves him distinct and singular. He was martyr for a lie; a lie, too, which, by any supposition, must inflict a fatal and certain penalty; for, if discovered, it must blacken his moral character, and if successfully concealed, it must be the death of his fame.

CARLYLE.

———◆———

I HAVE just finished Thomas Carlyle's last book, entitled, "Past and Present," and it has so filled my mind, that I must try to give my impressions of it. My admiration of this book is disinterested, for I am not of those who make Carlyle the god of their idolatry; yet, I trust, I am not insensible to the merits of so original a thinker, and so profound a critic. I have read all his productions; many of them with unmingled delight; and none of them, without appreciation of his extraordinary powers. To make allusion only to a few; his biography of Schiller; his comments on the life and writings of Richter; his analysis of Goëthe, are so fraught themselves with inventive genius, as to be creations, rather than criticisms, such as almost place the writer on a level with the great authors whom he reviews. With these I need hardly specify his most pathetic and eloquent "Essay on Burns;" a genuine and manly estimate of a most genuine and most manly poet. A position of Carlyle's own is, that to judge truly of faults, you must have entered fully into the excellence of your author; and this position he has nobly himself exemplified in his estimate of big-hearted Burns, the bard that " walked the mountain side in glory and in joy." But Carlyle has peculiarities, which no admiration can render pleasing to me. If some will call me conventional for such repugnance, I cannot help it. So it is in me, and I only show my improvement by Carlyle's lessons, by honest expression. It seems to me that Carlyle defies sheer force, and that he is intolerant, not merely to pretension, but to weakness. His views of man often appear to me exceedingly limited, and so also his ideas of good and evil. With most eloquent eulogies on genuineness, he does not much respect individual independence. The genuineness that he approves, is one which makes impression by some strong peculiarity; one which can maintain its right by power. Other than this he does not praise; nay, on humble men, who do the best they can in common ways, he pours out most scalding sarcasm, and most bitter ridicule. Carlyle would have the lower minds not merely subjects, but worshippers, and heroes should be their gods. To this worship I never can bend; I admire great souls, but I will not forsake my own; in my adoration I would fain aspire directly to the Creator of great souls. From a great many points in Carlyle's philosophy I sincerely dissent, but, within limits, desire to be a learner from Carlyle's teaching. That he is a man of a vigorous and earnest mind, I believe; that he is a man of a tranquil and catholic one, I doubt. His later style is not to be praised; enough, if it be borne; and nothing can more evince the value which is set on Carlyle's thoughts, than the endurance of his style. It is not English, and I know not what else it is. His terms, singly, to be sure, are Anglo-Saxon; but to what dialect his sentences belong, let philosophers determine. Still, let no one turn away from his odd and grotesque expression; let no one, on this account, cast aside a book of Carlyle's, or he will throw away a husk, which contains a very precious kernel. I have mastered his vocabulary, and find a wisdom in his words, which would repay twenty times the labor These exceptions are made in perfectly cordial temper; and now I will proceed to tell you all I can in a short space about the work I have already mentioned. As a literary composition, it has Carlyle's power and his defects; but its aim is directly practical, and its tone is impressively serious.

It is divided into four books. The first is entitled

the " Proem." It is a picture of English society in its present ominous condition, and is the deepest voice of advice and warning, which has come forth from the groaning heart of that sick and struggling country. There is a prophet-like depth in its tone of complaint, and a prophet-like energy in its indignant denunciation ; withal, it has modulations of sweetness and pity.

Book the second, is designated " The Ancient Monk." It resuscitates a fragment of the middle ages, with that picturesque vitality, in which Carlyle has no equal and no rival. This book is founded on an old MS., some time since discovered in England by the " Camden Society," containing a memoir of one Samson, abbot of the monastery of St. Edmundsbury in the twelfth century; Edmund was a generous Saxon Englishman, who, beloved by his people, and murdered by the Danes, became a saint. Three centuries after his death, his shrine was hung with riches, and a monastery existed under his patronage, with one of the broadest estates in the nation. Carlyle, in an eloquent character of St. Edmund, draws a beautiful picture of a good landlord. A certain indolent abbot, Hugo, not averse to prayer, but very much to work, gets the estate of the community into a sad embarrassment; but happily abbot Hugo took into his head to make a pilgrimage to Canterbury; and more happily abbot Hugo died on the way. A certain stout-souled monk, Samson, a man after Carlyle's own heart, is elected abbot; and, fortunately, a certain minute observer, Jocelin, wrote a chronicle. This Jocelin is also beloved of Carlyle, and in his endearment he calls him Bozzy — that is in a small way — for a Boswell is very gracious in the eyes of Carlyle, when there is a Dr. Johnson behind him. Abbot Samson sets to work like a man; reforms with radical energy, clears the house of drones, clears the estates of debts, and clears the vicinity of Jews. Abbot Samson has manifold occupations; he is governor, steward, judge, priest, and legislator; but abbot Samson is equal to them all. Abbot Samson has troubles with his monks, which he subdues by a wise and gentle courage; and that courage does not blench even in contest with the dauntless Cœur de Lion. The abbot had a wealthy ward, whom the king would marry otherwise, than the abbot deemed to be for her good. The king, by letter, requests that abbot Samson will give her as he directs. Abbot Samson replies with deep humility, that she is already given.

New letters from Richard, of severer tenor, were answered with new humilities, with gifts and entreaties; with no promise of obedience. Richard's ire is kindled; messengers arrived at St. Edmundsbury, with emphatic messages to obey or tremble. Abbot Samson, wisely silent as to the king's threats, makes answer ; " The king may send, if he will, and seize the ward ; force and power, he has to do his pleasure, and abolish the whole abbey ; I never can be bent to wish this that he seeks, nor shall it by me be ever done ; for there is danger lest such things be made a precedent of, to the prejudice of my successors. *Videat Allessemus.* Let the Most High look on it. Whatsoever things shall befall, I shall patiently endure. Richard swore tornado oaths, worse than our army in Flanders, to be revenged on that proud priest. But, in the end, he discovered, that the priest was right, and forgave him, and even loved him. The chronicle breaks off abruptly, and Carlyle closes the book with a fine chapter on the rise and progress of art and literature.

Then comes book the third, on " The Modern Worker." In this we have the philosophy of modern England ; and the philosophy is as grand as the subject. This is somewhat different from Jack-a-dandy Lester's, and his bottled pop and small beer declamations on the " Glory and the Shame of England." Carlyle does not conceal the shame of the age, but denounces it with a thunder voice ; its atheism, its mammonism, its dilettantism, its pretensions, its quackeries, its cants, its want of high and noble soul, its selfishness, its vain and idle aristocracies, its devouring monopolies, its naked and starving toilsmen, its pleasure-seeking and pleasure-loving lords. The topics here simply indicated, are rung out in Carlyle's huge diction, as if on the booming of St. Paul's great bell. But he gives the glory, as well as the shame. He notes the force of principle and of purpose, that lies in the silent depths of English character, and the evidence it leaves in the world; not in speech, but deeds; not in theories, but things. "The English," he says, "are a dumb people. They can do great acts, but not describe them. Like the old Romans, and some few others, their epic is written on the earth's surface; England her mark! It is complained, that they have no artists; one Shakspeare, indeed; but for Raphael, only a Reynolds; for Mozart, nothing but a Mr. Bishop; not a picture, not a song. And yet they did produce one Shakspeare. Consider how the element of Shaksperean melody does lie imprisoned in their nature; reduced to unfold itself in mere cotton mills, constitutional government, and such like; all the more interesting, when it does become visible, as even in such unexpected shapes it succeeds in doing!" * * Again: "Of all nations in the world at present, we English are the stupidest in speech, and wisest in action. As good as a dumb nation, I say, who cannot speak, and have never yet spoken — spite of the Shakspeares and Miltons, who show the possibilities that are. O Mr. Bull, I look into that surly face of thine with a mixture of pity and laughter, yet also with wonder and veneration. Thou complainest not, my illustrious friend, and yet I believe the heart of thee is full of sorrow, of unspoken sadness, seriousness, profound melancholy, (as some have said), the basis of thy being. Unconsciously, for thou speakest of nothing, this great universe is great to thee. Not by levity of floating, but by stubborn force of swimming, shalt thou make thy way. The fates sing of thee, that thou shalt many times be thought an ass and a dull ox, and shalt, with a godlike indifference, believe it. My friend, and it is all untrue ; nothing falser in point of fact ! Thou art of those great ones, whose greatness the small passers-by do not discern. Thy very stupidity is wiser than their wisdom. A grand *vis inertiæ* is in thee ; how many grand qualities unknown to small men. Nature alone knows thee, acknowledges the bulk and strength of thee ; thy epic, unsung in words, is written in huge characters on the face of this planet, sea moles, cotton trades, railways, fleets and cities, Indian empires, Americas, New Hollands, legible throughout the solar system.''

Carlyle enlarges, with soul-stirring exultation, on the glory of labor, on the blessedness of work. "Blessed,''

he says, " is he who has found his work ; let him ask no
other blessedness.   He has a work, a life-purpose ; he
has found it, and will follow it."   And here is a grand
picture of what work can do : "And again hast thou
valued patience, courage, perseverance, openness to
light, readiness to own thyself mistaken, to do better
the next time ?   All these, all virtues — in wrestling
with the dim brute powers of Fact, in ordering of the
fellows in such wrestle, there, and elsewhere not at all,
thou wilt continually learn.   Set down a brave Sir
Christopher in the middle of black ruined stoneheaps —
of foolish, unarchitectural bishops — red tape officials —
idle Nell-Gwin Defenders of the Faith — and see whether he will ever raise a St. Paul's Cathedral out of all
that, yea or no !   Rough, rude contradictors, are all
things and persons, from mutinous masons, and Irish
hodmen, up to idle Nell-Gwin Defenders, to blustering
red-tape officials — foolish, unarchitectural bishops. All
these things and persons are there, not for Sir Christopher's sake and his cathedrals ; they are there for
their own sake mainly !   Christopher will have to con-
quer and constrain all these — if he be able.   All these
are against him.   Equitable Nature herself, who carries
on her mathematics and architectories, not on the face
of her, but deep in the hidden heart of her.   Nature
herself is but partially for him ; will be wholly against

him, if he constrains her not! His very money, where is it to come from? The pious munificence of England lies far-scattered, distant, unable to speak, and say ' I am here ' — must be spoken to before it can speak. Pious munificence, and all help, is so silent, invisible, like the gods; impediments, contradictions manifold are so loud and near! O, brave Sir Christopher, trust thou in those, notwithstanding, and front all these; understand all these, by valiant patience, noble effort, insight, by man's strength, vanquish and compel all these — and, on the whole, strike down victoriously the last top-stone of that Paul's edifice; thy monument for centuries; the stamp ' Great Man ' impressed very legibly on Portland-stone there!"

The afflictive evils, that cry in England for remedy, are again and again referred to in all the chapters of this impressive section of the work, and warning repeated upon warning to apply the remedy, and to apply it directly.

The nature of the remedy in the author's mind is more clearly indicated in the fourth and last book, which he names the " Horoscope." First, the Corn Laws must go. That is now not a conjecture, but a certainty; not a prophecy, but a fact. Supposing the Corn Laws abolished, and the nation ensured on a course of prosperity, that possibly might continue for twenty years. At the close of that period, if nothing else be done in the mean time, the miseries, which now oppress the millions, would be found again with aggravated malignity. To avert this terrible result, what must be done, that the future, not only be safe, but progressive? The whole people must be educated. That is the radical amelioration, the basis of every other improvement. Systematic immigration must be established: This will relieve the labor-market at home, and extend the consuming-market abroad. Labor needs in some way a better organization, and the results of labor a more equitable distribution. And withal, higher sentiments must govern every class of society, not the Utilitarian, but one of more faith, and more ideality. The wisest must rule; industry must have dignity; the relations of life must have more elements of performance: both the landed and the gifted must recognize the sacredness of their trusts, and be faithful to them. These things being accomplished, England will be renovated for a new race of glory; if neglected, England's days are numbered. But the author is full of hope; he believes that the moral strength of England will come resistlessly to the task, and that his country will vindicate her might in this hour of fierce trial. Having an earnest hope in himself, he breathes it into others, and in this lyric-like strain he closes the work: " Unstained by wasteful deformities, by wasted tears and hearts' blood of men, or any defacement of the pit, noble, fruitful labor, growing ever nobler, will come forth, the grand sole miracle of man; whereby man has risen from the low places of this earth, very litterally into divine heavens. Ploughers, Spinners, Builders, Prophets, Poets, Kings, Brindleys and Goëthes, Odins and Arkwrights, all martyrs and noble men, and gods are of one grand host immeasurable, marching ever forward since the beginning of the world. The enormous, all-conquering, flame-crowned host; noble every soldier in it; sacred and alone noble. Let him who is not of it hide himself; let him trouble for himself. Stars at every button cannot make him noble; sheaves of Bath-garters, nor bushels of Georges; nor any other contrivance, but manfully enlisting in it, valiantly take place and step in it. O Heavens, will he not bethink himself? he too is so needed in the Host! it were so blessed, thrice blessed, for himself, and for us all! In hope of the last Partridge and some Duke of Weimer, among our English Dukes, we will be patient yet awhile.

> ' The future hides in it
> Good hap and sorrow;
> We press still thorow,
> Naught that abides in it
> Daunting us'—Onward.' ''

The several topics of this work, in name, seem very distinct and separate from each other, but in spirit they have a vital connection with each other, and form a complete unity in the whole. No period in the life of a nation is independent, no period stands by itself and alone; every period reproduces history, and is modified by influences which history carries onward. Thus, to understand the present complex nature of English society, we must trace how many elements have entered into its formation; and how these elements have been combined and developed in the progress of events. Not the least important elements in the constitution of English civilization, as of European civilization generally, were the feudal and the ecclesiastical. The Baron and the Monk for some centuries gave the the law, and shared dominion. Their persons may have disappeared from our modern forms, but the spirit of the Past never entirely dies; nor is that of Baron and of Monk extinct even in an age of cotton mills. To understand, therefore, even an age of cotton mills, in a country where the Baron and the Monk had lived, we must not exclude them from our consideration, or else, we shall have but an imperfect estimate. Carlyle, therefore, with that sagacious insight, which distinguishes his genius, passes in review before us, The Ancient Monk, to prepare us for The Modern Worker. The civiliza-

tion of chivalry and church has not departed even ex-
ternally from England, before the civilization of manu-
factures and commerce had attained no mean degree of
power. Now, that *arms* are sinking beneath *tools*, and
the *breviary* behind the Ledger-Book, there is yet the
result of a social condition, in which heterogeneous
principles have been at work, that have never coalesced
with the disorder and disease, which are the inevitable
consequences of such a state. But the crisis is come;
and now the problem is to get through it, to avoid a
fatal termination, and to start anew with increased and
recovered health. The difficulty is, to reconcile interests without destroying them : to lose nothing which
may be a means of true elevation ; to harmonize all the
social elements into unity and strength. Two points,
however, press with dire necessity ; and whatever else
be thought of in later speculation, these must be
attended to *instanter*. First, the people must be fed ;
secondly, they must be taught ; and these things can
brook no delay. Much may be done, if men will think
seriously ; much may be done by earnest purpose ; by
friendly combination, by honest compromise ; and
there is one hope in a tendency, which is growing
either from increase of principle, or the pressure
of the times ; and that is, men incline less to fac-

tion and more to truth — and hope the clouds will pass and leave all fertility behind them ; and if England is never again to be merrie, let her at least be prosperous.

SAVAGE AND DERMODY.

———◆———

SAVAGE is commonly connected with Chatterton, but except in the accident of their poverty, I could never, for my own part, find out any resemblance. As a man, Chatterton was of austere demeanour, and as a poet he was of the highest powers; but Savage as a man was extremely social, and as a poet was not greatly beyond mediocrity. Chatterton died rather than ask relief: Savage did not, indeed, solicit relief, he commanded it. All beings, however, have their use in God's creation. Savage has had his. He has been made an occasion for a piece of most beautiful and eloquent composition. Some men owe their fame to being the subject of a great biographer; and others to being the biographers of great subjects. Boswell has become famous in his Life of Johnson; and Savage has gained celebrity by the finely written record which has been left of him by Johnson. Nothing is more evident in this composition

than the fact, that the feelings of private friendship and
a remembrance of common misfortune broke the scourge
of criticism.   The poems of Savage may have merit;
but they assuredly have not that merit which could pro-
pitiate the maligner of Milton, and the depreciator of
Gray.   Savage was the outcast of society, and Johnson,
with the rough benignity of his nature, took him to his
heart; precisely on a principle similar to that which
caused him to carry a sick and unfortunate girl, through
Fleet Street, to a refuge.

"The Wanderer" of Savage is a very remarkable
production; the more remarkable when we consider the
circumstances in which it was composed.   Stanzas of
it were often written upon cobblers' stalls, and sometimes whole passages were indited in a pauper-lodging.
One special quality of the poem is the extreme purity,
and moral elevation of sentiment, contrasted with his
own practical conduct.   The following lines are worthy
of notice because Dr. Johnson quotes them:

> "To fly all public care, all venal strife,
>   To try the still compared with active life;
>   To prove by these, the sons of men may owe
>   The fruits of bliss to bursting clouds of woe;
>   That even calamity, by thought refined,
>   Inspirits and adorns the thinking mind."

And again :

" By woe, the soul to daring action swells,
   By woe, in plaintless patience it excels ;
   From patience, prudent, clear experience springs,
   And traces knowledge through the course of things ;
   Thence hope is formed ; thence, fortitude, success,
   Renown ; whate'er men covet or possess."

" The Bastard," another poem of his, is eulogized by the same stern critic. On the first publication it created a mighty rout. His unnatural mother, who published her own shame, and detested with a kind of hellish madness, the poor wretch who sprung from that shame, was scared by it wherever she went ; it was before her every where,. as a sentence of terror and damnation. It was quoted in her hearing, it was left open for her reading ; and the young man whom she first rejected, and then tried to hang, became her own moral executioner. The following lines have always affected me ; they touch a chord of sorrow, most musical and most melancholy :

" No mother's care
Shielded my infant innocence with prayer ;
No father's guardian hand my youth maintained,
Called forth my virtues, or from vice restrained."

If Johnson's estimate of Savage is an error, it is an error on the right side. It may be indulgent, but the unfortunate require indulgence. It may be merciful, but it is the criminal who have need of mercy. In some of his criticisms, Johnson has been nefariously unjust; but his charity, in the "Life of Savage," covers a multitude of sins. "For his life or his writings," he says, "none who consider his fortune will think an apology either necessary or difficult. If he was not always sufficiently instructed in his subject, his knowledge was at least greater than could have been obtained by others in the same state. If his works were sometimes unfinished, accuracy cannot reasonably be expected from a man oppressed with want, which he has no hope of relieving, but by speedy publication. The insolence and resentment of which he is accused, were not easily to be avoided by a great mind irritated by perpetual hardships, and constrained hourly to return the spurns of contempt, and repress the insolence of prosperity; and vanity may surely be readily pardoned in him to whom life afforded no other comfort than barren praises and the consciousness of deserving them." One of his latest and greatest faults, was that of keeping the Bristol merchants out of their comfortable beds with most eloquent and glorious talking; but the sin was surely not so grave, that for a mere trifle he should be left to die in a Bristol gaol.

Similar to Savage in some respects, different in others, was the Irish versifier, Dermody. He was one of those precocious spirits that at first excite astonishment, that are praised and puffed and glorified, that disappoint those who patronize them, that are idolized by those who bring them forward to desert them, that are wondered at for a while and deserted forever. Dermody as a boy was marvellous: Dermody as a man was nothing. His life is written by a good natured person of the name of Raymond, who, with a benevolent generosity that does him honor, often relieved his sufferings and allayed his hunger. I speak now of general recollections and impressions, which the reading of that life has left upon my mind. Dermody was an Irishman, and, as well as I can remember, he was the son of a drunken schoolmaster in Clare or Kerry. This schoolmaster did not treat his son well, but if he gave him scanty food, he crammed him plentifully with Greek and Latin. He was put into the Latin Accidence when he was but four years of age, and he ran away from his father when he was scarcely eleven. He accompanied a carrier to Dublin, and in the city's mass, he lost his conductor. He was found at a bookstall, reading Greek authors with a fixed interest, a queer compound of the careless boy and the well-trained scholar. He was first employed by an old man who sold second-hand books in a cellar, to indoctrinate his son in Latin. Dermody was then promoted to a shop above ground, to sell books to the students of the University, and to criticise them as he sold. From this he was taken by the pedantic and the wealthy; handed about from party to party, as the newest prodigy; taught to drink much and to sit long, and when at last incorrigible in the vices into which his patrons had initiated him, he was turned adrift upon the world. Merit sometimes droops and dies for the want of encouragement, but this was not the case with Dermody. Lady Moira, when he was utterly deserted, held out to him a most generous attention. She placed him with an able man to complete his education. Dermody, instead of minding his studies, dwindled his time away in the village tavern — and in writing verses on the village tailor and the village barber. The Lady Patroness at last disgusted, dismissed him, with a small sum of donation and a great deal of advice. Subsequently, he procured an Ensign's commission, and, to his honor it must be said, that in war he conducted himself with the bravery of a soldier, and in peace with the propriety of a gentleman. Having sold his commission, he was again thrown on the world, and after some alternations of poverty and extravagance, he closed his career in a solitary hut in England. Two friends found him here n a dying state. " He had scarce power left," his biographer says, " to express the grateful sentiments which their visit inspired. The words faltered on his parched lips ; his eyes became filled with tears, and being unable to utter the strong feelings which labored in his breast, he sunk again into the melancholy position in which they had discovered him, and continued silent for a considerable time."

The deserted appearance of the house, better calculated indeed, for the retreat of robbers, than the abode of a dying person, gave his situation the last touches of tragic misery. " Thank God," he exclaimed, " for this friendly visit ; I thought I had given the whole world, and you in particular, cause to forget me." The caution was needless ; his past sins were buried in the recollection of present wretchedness, and he had little to dread from the chidings of those who had now to perform only the few last offices of friendship. When his disorder allowed him to enter for a moment into conversation, he assumed a spirit, which, though faint, was yet mingled with the eccentricity that had on almost every occasion marked his character, and which was equally observable on trivial as on important matters. A violent fit of coughing having attacked him — " That hollow cough," said he, " rings out my knell." The comforts which his situation required and admitted, were procured for him. His two friends had arranged for him a pleasant lodging on the most delightful part of Sydenham Common; whither, with a careful nurse, he was to be removed on the following day. Money was given for all his immediate wants, and his benefactors, intending to call the next morning, had hoped for him some declining hours of calm transition to the grave. That same evening, however, Dermody expired, when he was twenty-seven years and six months of age.

Anecdotes are told of Dermody which possess considerable interest. Many of these are wonderful, and some of them are truly affecting. While a mere lad he translated a great part of Anacreon, with a fidelity that satisfied the austerest scholars, and with a fervor that might have been responded to by the warmest poet. Yet this youth of brilliant abilities by a thoughtless extravagance, subjected himself to the necessity of begging subscriptions for his poems, and to the humiliation of being dismissed from the doors of those from whom he supplicated assistance. He has been found, at times, exhausted in a garret, weary from hopeless excursions, and his bleeding feet lacerated to the bone. A story is recorded of him which merits repetition for its extreme beauty. The first night on which he had left his father, he walked until he was weary. He then cast his eye around him for some hut, where he might have a chance of rest. Seeing a light a little distance off, he made for it. On entering a miserable dwelling he beheld a corpse on some shapeless boards, with a lone and haggard woman leaning over it. He had but two shillings in his pocket, he gave the poor women one ; he went a small distance onward, repented, returned and gave her the other. Stopping for a while at an old church, as he continued his journey, he composed a poem, of which the following verses are a portion :

" Here where the pale grass struggles with each wind,
   Pregnant with forms, the turf, unheeded lies ;
   Here the fat abbot sleeps, in ease reclined,
   And here the meek monk folds his modest eyes.
     The nun more chaste than bolted snow
     Mingles with the dust below,
     Nor capricious turns away ;
     Lo ! to the taper's tremulous ray,
     White veiled shades their frames disclose,
     Vests of lily, cheeks of rose ;
     In dim fancy's vision seen
     Alive, awake, they rush between."

The poem closes with such sweet and solemn verses as these :

" Near pebbled beds, where rivulets play,
   And linger in the beams of day ;

'Mid sods by kneeling martyrs worn,
Embrowned with many a horrid thorn :

   *   *   *   *   *   *

Wont the solemn bell to flow
In silver notes, prolonging slow,
Tides of matchless melody.

   *   *   *   *   *

Yes, let them slumber here at last,
Their tyrannies—their sufferings past,
And lend a venerable dread
To the lone abbey's rocking head.''

The manner in which he sometimes describes his condition, is at once amusing and affecting. Here is an instance :

" In a cold empty garret, contented I sit,
  With no sparks to warm me, but sparks of old wit :
On a crazy black stool, doleful ditties I sing,
And, poor as a beggar, am blest as a king.
Then why should I envy the great folks and proud,
Since God has given me what he took from the crowd ?
My pen is my sceptre, my night-cap my crown,
All circled with laurels, so comely and brown.
Nor am I so powerful as people may think,
For lo! like all kings, I can spill floods of — ink ;
Fight armies of mice, tear huge spiders at will,
And murder whole fleets with the point of my quill ! ''

A reference to Otway, Chatterton, and Savage, is not ungraceful :

> " Sweet as the shepherd's pipe, my Otway sung,
> And pity melted on his soothing tongue,
> Yet, mark his need, too dreadful to be told,
> Death clad in scorn, in penury, and cold,
> His meek, imploring eyes, forever close,
> The Muse alone, poor partner of his woes.
> Sweet Chatterton, preferred in early prime,
> The steepest paths of noblest verse to climb,
> By felons spurned, illustriously died,
> And viewed this curst epitome of pride.
> Ill-fated Savage ! what could manhood bear
> Of cruel want, of agony severe —
> Of patient care, that springs a silent mine,
> What could it suffer — what that was not thine ? "

And thus, he most pathetically speaks of himself :

> " Me, hapless youth, the fury-troubles tear,
> Me from the Muses' rosy bosom wean :
> Dim streams my glance o'er sorrow's dreary scene —
> Dark to my sight Parnassian charms appear !   .
> Damp each bold ardor, each enthusiast fire,
> Sad-weeping o'er my song all-pensive laid,
> Or, haply roused from lethargies of woe ;
> Still, by new forms more terrible, dismayed,
> Harsh-featured penury and cares combined,
> Tearing with tiger-fang my tortured mind."

I close these desultory scraps from one who longed
for fame but lived for folly, with a short poem entitled
an " Ode to Frenzy ; "

> " Stabbed by the murderous arts of men,
>   My heart still op'd with many a wound,
> I pour the agonizing strain,
>   And view thee with deliriums round :
> Thy choicest tortures now prepare —
> O Frenzy ! free me from despair !
>
>   Thy visionary darkness shrouds
>   The tender brain in rayless clouds ;
>   Thy slow and subtle poison steals
>   Till abdicated Reason reels —
>   Then rising wild in moody trance
>   Quick, thy pale-visaged fiends advance.
>
> I burn, I throb, my pulses beat,
>   I feel thy rankling arrows now,
>   They tremble in my bleeding brow —
> And pierce reflection in his filmy seat ;
>   In heights of pain my heart is tost
>   And all the meaner sorrows lost.
>
> Who now will fear the puny sting of woe ?
>   Who start, disordered, at the phantom Death ?
> I mock the childish tears that trickling flow,
>   I smile at pangs, my softest pang beneath ;
> The canker grief, that silent eats, be thine —
> The noble ecstasy — be mine.

The hurried step — the pregnant pause severe —
   The spectred flash of sense — the hideous smile —
The frozen stare — Revenge's thrilling tear —
   The awful start, sharp look and mischief's secret wile ;
These are the proud demoniac marks I claim,
Since grief and feeling are the same ;
Then all thy racks sublime prepare,
And free me — Frenzy, from Despair !''

THE NEW YORK PUBLIC L
REFERENCE DEPARTMEN

This book is under no circumstanc
taken from the Building

form 410

Check Out More Titles From HardPress Classics Series In this collection we are offering thousands of classic and hard to find books. This series spans a vast array of subjects – so you are bound to find something of interest to enjoy reading and learning about.

Subjects:
Architecture
Art
Biography & Autobiography
Body, Mind &Spirit
Children & Young Adult
Dramas
Education
Fiction
History
Language Arts & Disciplines
Law
Literary Collections
Music
Poetry
Psychology
Science
…and many more.

Visit us at www.hardpress.net